Managing Your Career in a Changing Workplace

Jane Ballback
Jan Slater

Richard Chang Associates, Inc.
Publications Division
Irvine, California

Managing Your Career in a Changing Workplace

Jane Ballback
Jan Slater

Library of Congress Catalog Card Number 96-85724

ISBN 1-883553-76-8

First edition

The individuals and events in the case stories throughout this book are real. Names have been changed to protect their privacy.

RICHARD CHANG ASSOCIATES

Richard Chang Associates, Inc.
Publications Division
15265 Alton Parkway, Suite 300
Irvine, CA 92618
(800) 756-8096 (714) 727-7477 Fax (714) 727-7007

Acknowledgments

This book has been fifteen years in the making. We kept waiting for the *"right"* time to begin the writing process. That time never seemed to come, so our first acknowledgments are to Richard Chang and his many talented associates for moving this process along.

We taught ourselves this career development content through our own career and life experiences, by reading a wide variety of business, psychological, financial planning, and career books, and through our partnership of many years with Dr. Ann Coil, a creative and talented program developer and writer.

Our *"real"* teachers, though, were the thousands of clients who attended our workshops and visited our offices with their career challenges and dilemmas. Just when we thought we had heard it all, we would meet someone who had a new and unique story and had the courage and desire to learn something new about themselves and the world of work.

In addition, we would like to thank the many organizations who allowed us to come into their environments to assist in making their specific situation a win-win for everyone involved.

Last, but not least, thanks to Steve and Dennis for their unfailing support of us and the work that we do.

Additional Credits

Edited by Ruth Stingley

Reviewed by Denise Jeffrey

Graphic Layout by Christina Slater

Cover Design by John Odam Design Associates

Preface

Today we are faced with constant changes and increasing challenges that affect our personal and professional lives. Depending on how we address these changes and challenges, they can either be obstacles to growth or opportunities for advancement.

The advantage will belong to those with a commitment to continuous and advantageous learning. The goal of the Publications Division of Richard Chang Associates, Inc. is to provide individuals and organizations with a variety of practical and innovative resources for continuous learning and measurable improvement results.

It is with this goal in mind that we bring you the *Personal Growth and Development Collection*. These books provide realistic and proven advice, techniques, and tools—on a wide range of subjects—to build performance capabilities and achieve lasting results in your personal and professional life.

We hope that once you've had an opportunity to benefit from the *Personal Growth and Development Collection*, and any of the publications available in our *Practical Guidebook Collection*, you will share your thoughts and suggestions with us. We've included a brief Evaluation and Feedback Form at the end of the book that you can fax or send to us.

With your feedback, we can continuously improve the resources we are providing through the Publications Division of Richard Chang Associates, Inc.

Wishing you successful reading,

Richard Y. Chang
President and CEO
Richard Chang Associates, Inc.

Contents

Chapter 1 Key Points

- 🔑 There is no more normal
- 🔑 It's never getting back to *"normal"*
- 🔑 It's not worth your effort to hang on for the ride or play *"catch-up,"* you need to get ahead of the pack

When Is It Getting Back to Normal?

1

Imagine that Monte Hall has chosen you to participate in a special business segment of *Let's Make A Deal*. You're up on stage, direct center, facing Door #1, Door #2, and Door #3. Behind one door is your current job, with all its semi-predictable requirements, deadlines, and benefits. Behind another is a juicy package, Monte intimates, with a high salary, an office with a view, a 401(k) retirement plan, and a bonus program to make you salivate. The remaining door holds yet a different opportunity, a self-employment schedule with both flexible hours and income.

Which do you choose? *"Time's running out,"* Monte urges. You squeeze your eyes shut and point at Door #3. It's the high-ticket job! You clap your hands wildly and jump in the air, but before you make it to the swivel chair, Monte whispers in your ear, *"Congratulations! But don't forget—they're downsizing next year."*

"He who does not look ahead remains behind."
Spanish proverb

There is No More Normal

Welcome to the world of work. It may appear to be recognizable, but it's definitely not the same as it was fifty years ago, twenty years ago, or even five years ago. We, the authors, have seen tremendous changes in the more than fifteen years we've been involved in the career development business. It is these changes that make managing your career, well, nothing short of a challenge. It's not cut-and-dry. But once you understand how the vast changes in the world of work impact you in your particular cubicle, you can begin to take charge of your own career instead of letting the work world work you over.

> *Marcia Rodriguez, one of our clients who was a secretary for a large company, saw the writing on the wall when the company began a series of layoffs. She didn't want to follow in the footsteps of her colleagues who had been given their walking papers and who were now frantically searching for employment. "Some of my friends thought they'd have this job for life," she said. Although her heritage was Hispanic, Marcia enrolled in Spanish classes to master the correct way to speak and write Spanish. Now more marketable, she was ready for whatever would come. She heard through the grapevine that the company was creating an international division that would do a great deal of work with Latin America. She marketed herself into a position as executive secretary to the President of the International Division.*

In the world of work, normal is no longer normal. It continually needs to be redefined, because the pace of change has increased, and it keeps increasing at a rate that makes most of us want to yell *"Stop!"* New technology, our increasing ability to communicate, and our mobility all contribute to changes in the workplace.

But the bottom line is that we don't necessarily like change. We want to know what is expected of us and what we can expect, and if we are thrown a sharp curve that catches us unaware, we're floored. Surprise birthday parties may be fun, but surprise layoffs, surprise redefinitions of our jobs, and surprise changes in our benefits fall into a completely different category. You may not be thrilled with your particular job, but at least you know what it is. Or at least you think you do. Because what was normal for you yesterday may not be normal tomorrow.

What used to be normal is that people stayed with the same company until retirement, and they were repaid for their loyalty. The *"new"* normal is that the old rules don't exist. Companies may not value loyalty or at least not compensate for it. If layoffs occur, it may not matter that your nose was the closest to the grindstone for the longest time. And the clincher? This new way of thinking may become normal for generations to come.

So What Do You Do?

Good question. If change is going to be a constant in the world of work, how do you deal with it? The good news is that you do have a choice in the matter, and the magnitude of your success often depends on how you respond to the new changes in the world of work. You can either hang on for the ride, play *"catch-up,"* or get out ahead of the pack.

Hang on for the ride

There's a certain comfort to hanging on for the ride when you are faced with work changes. Partly due to our preconceptions of what work is and how we should be treated, we mistakenly think that everything will be okay if we just do the same thing or work

"There is no security on this earth. There is only opportunity."
Douglas MacArthur

> "We need to wake up from the American dream."
> Joe Dominguez and Vicki Robin

even harder at the same thing. One company told its employees it would be shutting down within the year. The employees responded by doubling their work effort, which vastly increased productivity. But the sad moral of the story is that the extra work didn't make a bit of difference. The company still closed its doors. Had the employees channeled their energy into managing their own careers, the story would have had a much happier ending.

Play "catch-up"

Did you ever take a class that was a little beyond your comprehension? You'd try and try to master a certain concept, but when the light bulb finally switched on, your instructor was in the middle of explaining the next concept. You never felt caught up, at least not for very long. It's not that different in the work world. You might learn a new computer program or take a business class to keep abreast of the changes at work, but you're still not ready when your company decides to merge, downsize, or even change work processes. Stressful? Absolutely. You continually have to play *"catch-up"* to keep up.

Get ahead of the pack

Two clients of ours, Tim Morril and Rusty Herley, were both laid off from high-paying, low-skilled jobs, and wanted to find a job in Nevada that would allow them to work with their hands. "We also wanted a secure job that wouldn't lower our standard of living," they said. Their research led them to slot-machine repair in Laughlin. The job paid well, allowed them to use their mechanical expertise, and showed no signs of becoming obsolete. Moreover, as independent contractors, they could set their own hours and pay rates. It was a win-win situation for all involved.

Getting out ahead of the pack requires initiative on your part. You don't have to be a seer to move ahead, but it does take some knowledge and foresight, so knowing how the world of work is changing is essential to your venture. You have to learn how to unlock your career potential, do labor market research, and know how to market yourself. Our clients find it an exciting prospect, even exhilarating at times, because they finally gain control over something that monopolizes such a sizable chunk of their lives.

Is That It?

In a nutshell, yes. Change is inevitable. If you have yet to feel its effects in the workplace, you won't have to wait long. Companies change, jobs change, and your response to these changes determines your destiny.

How will you respond to the new world of work? Will you hang on for the ride, play catch-up, or get ahead of the pack? Read on. You'll learn how the major changes in the world of work play into your personal work life; you'll also discover strategies to parlay your talents into a career of your own choosing, a career that emphasizes viewing yourself as an *"independent contractor,"* whether you work for yourself or someone else. You can't afford to miss out.

"It is practically a law of life that when a door closes on us, another opens. The trouble is that we often look with so much regret and longing upon the closed door, that we do not see the one which is open for us." Anonymous

"Well, I'll be darned, maybe they are serious about restructuring."

Chapter 2 Key Points

🗝 Companies are shrinking in size

🗝 The *"old"* contract has been broken, making lifetime employment virtually obsolete

🗝 Jobs don't look the same anymore

🗝 To get ahead, you have to assess your own strengths, write your own contract based on your value, and market yourself

Where Is the Company You Used to Work For?

2

In the workshops we have conducted, we've heard employees comment countless times, *"It's not the same company. The company that hired me has changed."* And they're serious. Deadly serious. They don't mean that the company has been bought out; they're concerned over the fact that the company is different. It is smaller and leaner; the benefits look nothing like they used to; and the jobs have changed in scope, size, and title. It's like waking up to your mate after so many years and realizing that he or she looks and acts radically different from the person you married. It's downright scary.

The Case of the Shrinking Company

> *A financial institution located in a large metropolitan area laid off five hundred employees in one day. Not one hundred employees over the course of one year. Five hundred employees in one day! All five hundred were situated in the basement of the institution and primarily handled data-entry functions. However, one would think that if you took five hundred people and laid them off in one day, something would change, something wouldn't be able to function. Not in this scenario. Business proceeded as usual. Because the people in charge changed the nature of the way the work was done, five hundred people became superfluous.*

One of the major changes in the world of work is that the average size of American companies has decreased. This increasingly common phenomenon is one that alarms many employees. After all, who is going to pay the mortgage if you get laid off? Case in point: Pac Bell now serves twice as many customers with half as many people. You can bet the employees who were asked to leave didn't rejoice over that accomplishment.

What is behind this change? Why are companies shrinking? The reasons vary. Technology is a big one, since computers can take over much of what people routinely do—from taking orders at Taco Bell to guiding manufacturing machines. But technology isn't the only stimulus for this change. Other reasons include:

♦ An increased focus on productivity. Cost-cutting pressures make people analyze the work that needs doing, and often that means paring it down to the bare minimum. Reengineering efforts often result in a need for fewer employees.

♦ A reduction in the need for managers. Layers of management are being eliminated as companies opt for more hands-on management. In some instances, self-managed teams eliminate direct management altogether.

All this is good news for companies, and it's not necessarily all bad news for employees either. The trick is in figuring out how to become an indispensable member of your company—to get ahead of the pack.

Become a "preferred supplier"

Can you describe your job in detail? Don't recite your job description, which, by the way, is rather useless. Describe the functions of your job. What exactly do you do? If you understand the core functions of your job, you can determine whether your job or parts of it are indispensable. For example, if a core function of your job is to assemble a widget, you are entitled to worry about a machine replacing you. But if most of the core functions of your job are still essential and you are competent, you are a preferred supplier.

Part of being a preferred supplier means continually assessing your job. What is indispensable today may not be tomorrow, so keep your finger on the pulse of your organization and your contribution to it. If you can predict that your job is headed toward the useless category, do some research and identify what is important to your company. Learn new skills or market yourself into a new position that is of value.

Another option to consider is becoming an external supplier. For example, Marcia Rodriguez, the bilingual executive secretary we mentioned in the previous chapter, had thought about leaving her company and marketing her services to different corporations.

"Life is not the way it's supposed to be. It's the way it is. The way you cope with it is what makes the difference."
Virginia Satir

While she chose to remain an internal preferred supplier, she also had the option to become an external one. Keep all your options open.

What Happened to the Gold Watch?

At one of our workshops, we encountered a man who had been with the same company for fifty-three years. Fifty-three years! We made him say it three times. In today's society, that is practically unheard of. People used to stay at a corporation for life, but today there is no such thing as a lifetime employee. Employee longevity and business have become unlikely bedfellows.

It wasn't always so. The old contract *(and we're not speaking about union contracts here)* was an unspoken promise that most employees understood the moment they began work. *"You won't get rich working here,"* the old contract vowed, *"but we will take care of you, and you will have a job for life as long as you show up for work every day, keep your nose clean, don't make too many enemies, and do as you're told."* It was an appealing guarantee. You could see it in the pictures of long-time employees on the wall, read it on the perfect-attendance awards, and understand its significance when the perks were handed out at retirement parties.

Over the years that contract has been revoked, and it is now in the process of being rewritten. The new contract between employers and employees is also unspoken, but all points ring with definite clarity:

"We need employees who are eager to stay, but ready to go."
Bill Walsh, CEO of General Electric

- ◆ There is no job security.
- ◆ You work here as along as you add value.
- ◆ You need to figure out how to add value.
- ◆ You work here as long as there is work to do, and not a minute longer.

Build your own security

The breaking of the old contract and its subsequent revision foster insecurity. We see the ramifications of this scenario played out time and time again, especially in the lives of middle-aged and older workers who are laid off and have trouble competing for jobs with younger individuals who know how to play the game. How do you get around the insecurity that's indelibly written into the new contract? By building your own security. It's one way to successfully handle contract negotiations.

Building your own security involves pro-active marketing. If you followed the tips in the previous section, you know what it takes to become a preferred supplier. Make sure you analyze and assess your competencies at least once yearly. Then ask yourself:

♦ Is meaningful work still here?
♦ Am I provided the resources to do it well?
♦ Am I the best person to do it?
♦ Does my pay reflect my contribution?

If you answer yes to all these questions, your contract serves you well. If your work is not meaningful, you may be on the fast track out. Make yourself indispensable or look elsewhere. If you could do your work better with a new computer or additional training, negotiate for the supplies or education you need to be the best person for the job. Ditto with the compensation; negotiate if you feel you are worth much more than you are being paid.

"Easier said than done," you may grumble. And, certainly, it will take time and effort to adjust to the revised contract. But if it's in your best interest, consider it. The new contract does have one trump card, and that is the freedom to leave a company. Leaving your job under the old contract was a major breach, and prospective employers questioned any moves that weren't geographical in origin.

> "Destiny is not a matter of chance, it is a matter of choice; it is not a thing to be waited for, it is a thing to be achieved."
> William Jennings Bryan

Today's employers realize that employees aren't reprimanded for changing loyalties, and valuable employees are worth listening to. Become a valuable employee and you can participate in your own contract. Now isn't that more appealing than the proverbial gold watch?

> *One of our more progressive client companies makes employees go on one external job interview a year and report their results. It serves a double purpose. Employees learn to stay marketable (which is beneficial for both parties), and they also see whether the grass is greener on the other side. It's part of the new two-way contract: "You work here as long as you add value and as long as you find the work meaningful and worthwhile."*

Just Get the "Work" Done

> *One of our clients, a consulting group, realized that the old way of compartmentalizing jobs was stifling. "Projects don't get finished on time," one consultant complained, "because the same people get inundated with work from various projects all at once." The consulting group decided to get out of the box and set up a new system, whereby employees would join a "project team." The team would be responsible for seeing the project through from start to finish. When the project was near completion, the team members were responsible for choosing a different project team to join. The result? Work got done on time with less griping.*

Jobs, as we know them, are disappearing. A job, that is, that can be visualized as a tight box, with a bottom, four sides, and a lid. It comes with a particular description; and, while it has its limitations, it's a definite known. No surprises. If changes are made, and the lid is blown off, it will be replaced with a lid that sets new parameters for your job.

In business circles, that is the old way of looking at jobs. But actually, it's not that old: just over one hundred years, to be exact. It wasn't until the 1800s, when industrialization transformed work into jobs completed at a factory, that jobs came into existence. Before that, what ate up most of the day was work, work at whatever task needed to be accomplished—from milking the cows to building a barn. Today, many of the specialized tasks that became jobs are either obsolete or close to it, thanks to technology.

Companies also are waking up and realizing that jobs with their own set of job descriptions are limiting. If you place an employee in a specific job, what happens when you want that employee to do something outside of his job description? Write a new job description? *(Then you'd need to hire a person whose job was to constantly update job descriptions.)* Instead, companies just want to get the *"work"* done—to finish all the tasks that need to be finished.

It does makes sense. If you think about it, you've no doubt experienced how limiting that job box can be. No one wants to help you with your groceries, because that is the grocery clerk's domain, and he's nowhere to be seen. Or you've just paid for your purchases at a department store, when you notice that the salesperson overcharged you. You tell her it was on sale, but she says it didn't ring up that way and directs you to customer service on another floor. And, on the corporate level, think about the express package that doesn't get sent on time because it's the job of a person who's out sick.

Adapting to the "ex-job" environment

What does this mean to you? How should you respond to the changes in the job structure? Start by changing your way of thinking. Look at your *"job"* in terms of the functions you handle, the projects you complete, and the results you achieve. Become more well-

> "The rung of a ladder was never meant to rest upon, but only to hold a man's foot long enough to enable him to put the other somewhat higher."
> Thomas Huxley

connected within your organization, learn to be flexible, and market yourself. The more willing you are to do what needs to be done, the more you will get done. Need some additional ideas? Consider:

- seeking out and initiating projects

- reading journals

- going on-line

- attending conferences

- joining professional organizations

- making contacts in your organization for informal networking

These things don't come easy for everyone. On the one hand, you need to be task-oriented; on the other, you need to be a superb team player. If you're an analytical person, one who's primarily into number-crunching and data collection, you might cringe at ideas such as networking within your organization. Many of our clients fall into this category. We tell them that they won't get noticed unless they begin to crack out of their shells. It's okay to be an introvert, but you won't get ahead in any organization if you talk to nobody. Start with simple one-on-one interactions.

Where are you on the continuum? Know your strengths and what you bring to your company. Neither end of the spectrum is where you want to be, since you need both social and analytical skills to succeed. The key is to develop and work on your weak areas. Then you'll be one of the preferred suppliers your company calls when it wants work done.

Summary

The American company is changing its face and its behavior. Now leaner due to technology, a focus on productivity, and a reduced need for managers, it reveres loyalty in terms of productivity instead of longevity. And it's slowly changing the structure of work, replacing the *"job"* system with teams and an emphasis on getting work done.

All of which means that you, as an American worker, have to throw out your stereotypes of the American company and replace the old patterns of *"job behavior"* with workable solutions— recognizing your strengths, being pro-active in marketing yourself, and learning to fit your skills to your company's needs. The changes may be startling, but they also can serve as the push you need to get ahead of the pack.

"Congratulations, Fernbaugh. In just six months you've moved from an entry-level position to an exit-level position."

Chapter 3 Key Points

🗝 Contingency workers from all professions are flooding the marketplace

🗝 The work world is split between the *"haves"* and the *"have-nots"*

🗝 *"Technicians"* are in high demand

🗝 Workers are more mobile—they have the freedom to change whom they work for and where they work

Where Have All the Jobs Gone?

3

Something else is also happening on America's job scene. It's not enough that companies are changing the way they look at jobs; the labor market is right in the midst of its own major upheaval. Many full-time workers are being replaced; we're seeing the advent of a new job classification—the *"technician,"* along with the demise of some semi-skilled jobs; and droves of people are becoming more mobile in terms of what company they work for and where they work. These aren't mere predictions. They are happening already, and are transforming the way America does business. So hang onto your seats as we show you the remaining loops on the roller coaster of work change.

Contingency Workers Make the Cut

> *A large engineering consulting firm that handled a wide variety of projects hired many temporary employees on a consistent basis. Tired of paying the temporary employment fees, they created their own in-house, for-profit temporary agency. Anyone interested in working for the firm has two choices: apply at the firm itself or at their temporary agency. Walk through the contingency door, and you'll make more money on a daily basis for the length of any one project, and you'll receive minimum benefits. Apply in the traditional way, and you'll get full-time work plus benefits. Both are popular. The surprise ending to this example? Because the in-house agency sends its employees to work on projects at other firms, the contingency workers may have more job security than the traditional employees.*

Odds are that you work alongside a contingency worker, have one in the family, or are one yourself. Business researchers calculate that more than one-quarter of the American work force is made up of contingency workers. That number is expected to double in less than a decade. Whatever your mathematical abilities, you have to agree that contingency workers—freelancers, part-timers, or subcontractors hired to handle unexpected or temporary needs—are gaining ground in employment circles. Need more convincing? The largest employer in the United States is none other than a temporary agency.

The biggest reversal in the stereotyping of contingency workers is that they now hail from all levels of all professions. They're as likely to be architects or administrators as part-time bank tellers, clerical helpers, or dishwashers. One of our clients, a female accountant, not only became a contingency worker for a Big Six accounting firm by rearranging her schedule to work three days a week, but she also was made a partner.

Companies are often eager to hire temporary or part-time help, because they save money by not having to shell out benefits— medical insurance, sick-day pay, retirement plans, vacations, etc. It translates into major savings. And they only have to keep contingency workers as long as they need them, without hassling over pink slips and severance packages.

If you decide on contingency work, however, there is a way you can get benefits. You list with a temporary agency that provides the same perks that full-time workers take for granted. Companies pay more for such help, but they're guaranteed pre-screened, reliable workers. And often it's a way for companies to *"try out"* workers before they hire them as full-time employees. Both sides can win.

Some critics have a problem with a growing contingency work force. They say it can harm full-time employees, but that's not necessarily so. It is ludicrous to suggest that the entire work force become contingency workers. And, full-time employees could very well owe contingency workers a favor, because temporary or part-time workers don't feed from the welfare or unemployment troughs, and they often add to the stability of companies, which protects the jobs of full-time workers.

> "Instead of being a castle, a home for life for its defenders, an organization will be more like an apartment block."
> Charles Handy,
> The Age of Unreason

Contingent by choice

Not all contingency workers are so by choice. But for others, contingency work is well worth it. You have more flexibility, control, and usually higher pay. On the flip side, you do have to manage your money well, believe in your own value, and often market yourself. If you'd like to consider contingency work, but aren't sure whether or not you are cut out for it, take a few minutes and answer the questions that follow.

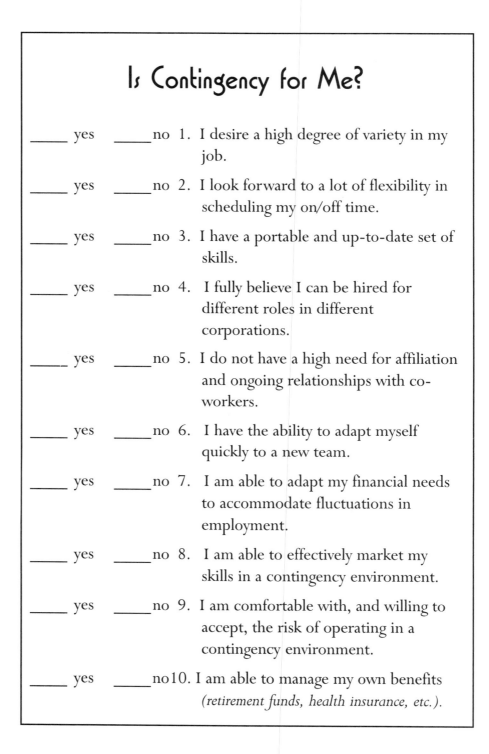

Is Contingency for Me?

_____ yes   _____ no 1. I desire a high degree of variety in my job.

_____ yes   _____ no 2. I look forward to a lot of flexibility in scheduling my on/off time.

_____ yes   _____ no 3. I have a portable and up-to-date set of skills.

_____ yes   _____ no 4. I fully believe I can be hired for different roles in different corporations.

_____ yes   _____ no 5. I do not have a high need for affiliation and ongoing relationships with co-workers.

_____ yes   _____ no 6. I have the ability to adapt myself quickly to a new team.

_____ yes   _____ no 7. I am able to adapt my financial needs to accommodate fluctuations in employment.

_____ yes   _____ no 8. I am able to effectively market my skills in a contingency environment.

_____ yes   _____ no 9. I am comfortable with, and willing to accept, the risk of operating in a contingency environment.

_____ yes   _____ no 10. I am able to manage my own benefits _(retirement funds, health insurance, etc.)._

If you answered yes to all or most of these statements, contingency work may be more than a viable alternative for you. It could be an avenue whereby you discover success in your chosen field. Take it into consideration; you do have more than 25 percent of America's work force behind you.

The Widening Gap Between the "Haves" and the "Have-Nots"

> A friend of ours, Katie Giordano, began her career as a secretary in a financial institution. Although not college-educated, she had enrolled in a computer school out of high school and took a few classes before she started in the world of work. Years later, rumor had it that her bank was downsizing. We called to offer her our support, but Katie wasn't the least bit nervous. "To tell you the truth, I have no guarantees," she told us. "But over the years I have taught myself programs that very few people know. And actually, I get calls from headhunters internationally. So if my bank doesn't want me, it won't be my choice to go, but neither will I be afraid." Katie is a good example of being both trade-school and self-educated in specialized skills that not only increased her income, but kept her immune from the traditional job-security worries.

America's work force is becoming increasingly polarized. In other words, it is being split into two very distinct categories—the *"haves"* and the *"have-nots."* The *"haves"* are individuals who have degrees, credentials, or special skills that catapult them into earnings of $40,000 or more per year. The *"have-nots"* lack degrees, credentials, or special skills, and usually end up with jobs in the service sector that pay less generously—somewhere around six dollars an hour.

"In the 90's temporary workers are handling not only routine tasks but also professional jobs. And these days more than 80 percent of temporary workers turn out to be so motivated and productive that they end up in permanent jobs."
Paul Burnham Finney

What's missing? Semi-skilled manufacturing jobs and middle-management positions are among those disappearing from the world of work, both which command salaries somewhere in the middle of the *"haves"* and the *"have-nots."* Travel agents are disappearing, because their commissions were taken away, and you can be on-line yourself. Bank tellers are in less of a demand than ATMs. And secretaries are being replaced with word processors. We discussed the reasons why jobs are disappearing in Chapter Two. What's left are the consequences for the American workers.

There is absolutely nothing wrong with jobs that pay six dollars an hour. We recall holding jobs that paid much less, and it was a great start for us and would be for anyone else. However, the bottom line is that it is not easy living on a limited income, much less raising a family on one. And what about your children *(if you have children)*? Will they be able to subsist on six dollars an hour *(and the inadequate benefits that usually accompany such positions)*, or will they be moving back in with you?

Moving toward the $40,000+ end

If you're in with the *"have-nots"* or the *"have-no-job"* category, we're not advocating that you drop everything and return to college to get your BA or post-graduate degree. In the brave new world of work, that might be an ultimate goal, but we know reality intervenes. Few people can afford that route, and some of those who can still might get stuck on the six-dollar end if they get their degrees in an obscure field or one that's glutted.

No, that's not the only path. You're going to look at the ads in your local paper, check out college catalogs, and look at extension courses. See what degrees and credentials are being offered. If you are in the middle of the spectrum, on the edge of the disappearing-job hole, seriously consider getting a degree or credential certificate, or training to learn a specialized skill that will edge you away from the abyss and closer to the haven of the *"haves."*

Wanted: A "Technician"

> *Librarians are losing their jobs due to cuts in library services. However, recently on the Internet, there was a job ad for an Internet librarian, someone who could classify and disseminate information on the Internet. Because of technology, this job exists. It's highly specialized and requires an independent worker. Only a "technician" could fill this job.*

Yes, jobs are disappearing. But new ones are also being created. We see this with the surge of need in the service sector. Labor-market predictions foresee a greater need for food-service workers, retail salespeople, and even gardeners. Another growth area is in the new job classification called *"technician."* Sixteen percent of the work force falls in this category; predictions place it at 20 percent in the future.

Technicians are independent workers with specialized skills. They are neither management nor labor. Their jobs arise out of technology, and they are more interested in using their skills than climbing the corporate ladder. The nature of their jobs vary— from the medical lab technician who draws your blood to the auto technician who diagnoses—and treats— your car's problems.

The challenge for technical workers in the world of work is trying to fit themselves into hierarchical organizations. It's not a good match. Their unwillingness to defer to management comes not from a sense of snobbery, but because they are too specialized to be adequately overseen. They do best as *"independent contractors,"* whether working for themselves or for an organization.

Even an organization as small as a dentist's office may need a technician. Steve, a laser technologist, works as a self-contractor for dental offices. He went to school for two years to learn his trade, and he now makes nearly as much money as some dentists.

The job is so specialized, no one but the technician knows how to do it.

If you are interested in becoming and/or succeeding as a technician, one of the fastest-growing sectors of the American work force, consider the following steps:

◆ Develop specialist skills, either through schooling or on-the-job training

◆ Do everything within your power to broaden those skills to make yourself more valuable

◆ Volunteer to work on bigger and better projects

The End of Company, Career, and Office Loyalty

The new mobility has kicked into gear. This last major change in the world of work has double meaning for workers: employees are freed from their allegiance to one company or career, and they are also given new options in where they work. The change can be either empowering or binding, depending upon how you look at it.

Mobility, in regard to loyalty, provides you with the freedom to move from company to company or career to career. The stigma is gone, because loyalty is no longer considered a yardstick of success. If you're a career- or company-jumper, your loyalty and stability are no longer questioned. It's what many people do, so you learn to market your experience instead of your allegiance— quite a liberating concept.

"Mobility is now the order of the day. That is terrifying and depressing news for those clinging to the corporate walls by their fingernails."
Jack Falvey

For those who are afraid of this change, it may be reassuring to know that there still will be *"lifers"* at many corporations. The only difference from the *"lifers of old"* is that the *"new lifers"* will have to prove their value just as often as the movers and shakers. It's all part of the new contract.

Going home to work

> *A large telecommunications company had 1,200 workers in one building. They decided to shut the building down and send everyone home to work. They weren't downsizing; they were saving money by eliminating office space. And what were the results six months down the line? Fifty percent of the employees had some difficulties with the transition. They missed the personal contacts. In response, the company built a satellite office for these folks. Twenty-five percent of the workers loved it. Their productivity soared, because they were able to get some "real work" done. And the remaining 25 percent just couldn't do it. They quit.*

Job mobility also offers more choices about where you work. Since many businesses are reducing or getting rid of typical office space, they have little choice but to send employees home to work. Other workers are starting their own home-based businesses. And still others spend part of their work week at home, accomplishing as much or more by eliminating their commute.

But working at home is not for everyone. Some people miss the social contacts at work, others procrastinate in the home environment, and still others don't have the space and/or the necessary equipment. A client of ours, a sales manager for a large manufacturing company, was visibly upset when his company dismantled his office and sent him home to work. Why? Because they took his secretary and his office. They were the trappings of success, and he felt inadequate without them.

You, on the other hand, might enjoy the freedom and flexibility. If you think working at home is an option you would like to pursue, complete the following questionnaire.

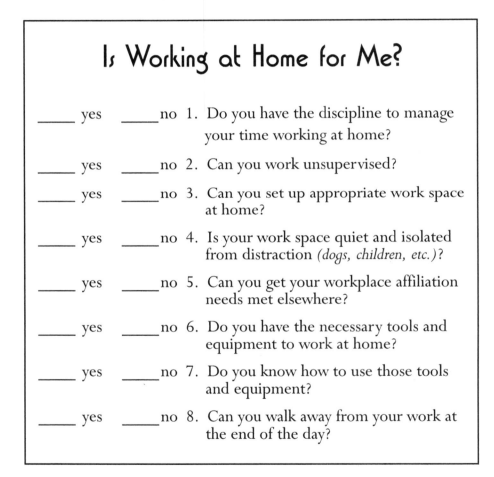

Is Working at Home for Me?

_____ yes _____ no 1. Do you have the discipline to manage your time working at home?

_____ yes _____ no 2. Can you work unsupervised?

_____ yes _____ no 3. Can you set up appropriate work space at home?

_____ yes _____ no 4. Is your work space quiet and isolated from distraction (*dogs, children, etc.*)?

_____ yes _____ no 5. Can you get your workplace affiliation needs met elsewhere?

_____ yes _____ no 6. Do you have the necessary tools and equipment to work at home?

_____ yes _____ no 7. Do you know how to use those tools and equipment?

_____ yes _____ no 8. Can you walk away from your work at the end of the day?

Scoring Key

Count your *"yes"* answers and see how you scored:

7-8: Working at home is a definite option for you. If your company gives you the option, you'd be a good candidate.

5-6: Working at home could still be a consideration, but you might try a trial run before making a commitment to do so. One or two days a week at home might be optimal for you.

Under 5: You may not be cut out for *"home"* work at this time. Try again at a later date.

A client of ours, Jacob Rahn, a sales manager for an office-furniture manufacturer, had an hour-long commute to his office. The company closed down the office and sent Jacob home with his computer. He still has to be out in the field with his salespeople; but, because of telecommuting, he now gets up at 6 a.m. instead of 4, feeds his kids breakfast, and takes them to school. Then he sits down to work. He goes to the gym on his lunch time, volunteers at his children's school, and coaches a soccer team. He finishes the same amount of work in less time due to telecommuting. And he has been rewarded with a greater amount of freedom.

Another way people work at home is by opening a home-based business. Eight million Americans opened a home-based business last year. Their average income before taxes was $49,000, and statistics reveal that 85 percent of them will succeed. Why the high success rate?

First of all, if you decide to open a home-based business, it is yours. That fact alone adds appreciably to the success rate, because you'll work harder at something if you profit from it. You're not punching the time clock for Company ABC; you are investing hours for you. Second, home-based businesses have low start-up costs.

"People can be divided into three groups: those who make things happen, those who watch things happen, and those who wonder what happened."
John Newber

Third, there is very low overhead. And the last, and main reason why home-based businesses succeed, is that you can start a home-based business while you are still working for someone else. In other words, you don't have to rely on your new business to make your living for you.

Would two success stories whet your appetite? One client of ours, a man in the path of layoff at a major utility company, bought one of those inflatable, bouncing castles that kids jump around in at birthday parties. He was dead tired at the end of his five-day work week, but on weekends he began to rent the castle to parents for their kids' parties. Soon he made enough money to buy a second one. When his company laid him off, he bought six more with his severance pay. Currently, he has more than replaced his $60,000 a year salary on a two-day work week, and he's now added popcorn and clowns to his business. It was hard work, and it took him two years, but he did it.

Another client, a pregnant woman in a high position at a bank, noticed the need for reasonably-priced maternity clothes. She started running a maternity-clothes rental business out of her home, renting maternity clothes for work and special occasions. She quit her job three months after starting this business, and she netted $110,000 her first year.

That does it for the major changes in the world of work. They are inherently neither good nor bad. They just are. But you can acknowledge their impact and start making your own moves that place you ahead of the pack. It's a far better choice than burying your head in the sand and hoping the world of work will revert back to its old way of doing things. That ain't gonna happen. You, on the other hand, are the only one who can take charge of your own career and make things happen.

Summary

We've described four major changes to the world of work that directly impact American workers. All will change the way America does business and will trickle down to change the way you do business.

♦ Contingency workers are on the rise. You've probably even been one at some time or another, and it may be a viable option for you now.

♦ The work world is becoming polarized, splitting into two distinct categories—the *"haves"* and the *"have-nots."*

♦ If you're in the *"have-not"* category, you may be able to bridge the gap by joining the ranks of *"technician"*—a new classification of those whose specialized technical skills place them in a category of their own.

♦ And finally, you've been given more freedom than ever before, freedom to change careers, companies, and even your place of work. As more Americans are going home to work for others or themselves, we're seeing a new liberation among American employees.

These changes may very well motivate you to rethink the direction of your career.

"Actually, I'm a waiter. I'm only doing this until I find a restaurant that suits my talents."

Chapter 4 Key Points

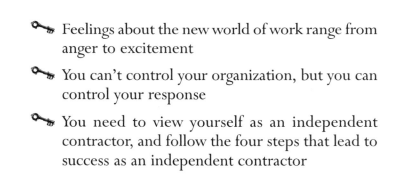 Feelings about the new world of work range from anger to excitement

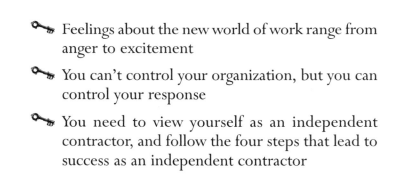 You can't control your organization, but you can control your response

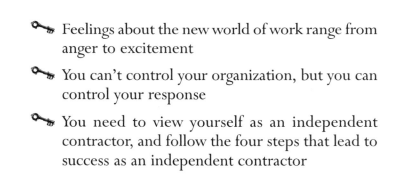 You need to view yourself as an independent contractor, and follow the four steps that lead to success as an independent contractor

Where Do You Go from Here?

4

You have entered uncharted territory—the new world of work. Like any explorer in an unknown land, you may feel a little lost, perhaps even hopeless, at times. However, many people have discovered that a better understanding of this new world leads them on a helpful detour through a tunnel of self-discovery toward a new area of freedom and self-sufficiency. The changes in today's workplace may have taken you by surprise, but they cannot be ignored. And, although you may not be able to control the new world of work, you can decide how you will respond to the challenges it presents.

Taking Control of What You Can

Few people react to the news about the world of work without emotion. Typical reactions range from anger and anxiety all the way to excitement and anticipation. *"What do you mean my benefits are going the way of the dinosaur?"* one person will rage, while another remarks, *"I can really see myself as a telecommuter. Maybe my company will allow me to do that."*

It is absolutely natural to have such feelings. *"How could this happen to me? The work world has betrayed me!"* may be their response. Other people see it as a minor inconvenience; still others find it to be motivational, a good kick in the pants, if you will.

The reality is that reactions differ. Perhaps those hardest hit are individuals who have been in the work force a number of years or employees who have been loyal to one company. They don't even see the changes *(because they can be quite subtle)* until they're struck down by a merger or layoff.

> *One of our client companies has many third-generation employees who are intensely loyal to the company. One particular employee, Laura Martin, had been with the company for thirty years before she was let go. "I just couldn't handle it," Laura remarked to us, "especially when I saw the picture of my grandfather on the company wall as I was walked out of the building." When her grandfather visited her the following week, she broke down at the dinner table. "I am so sorry," she told him. "I have disgraced you and the family and let you down. I am so angry at the betrayal of this organization." For Laura, it wasn't a clean break at all. She felt she had let the company down; they, in return, had betrayed her. Laura's reaction is not atypical.*

Getting beyond the feelings

If you are not closely tied to the apron strings of your organization, the new world of work may open the door to exciting new challenges and opportunities. A female CPA, tired of a long commute and the extra hours she put in at her company, attended one of our workshops and really took to the idea of contingency work. She applied at a temporary agency that specialized in accounting work and got herself a four-day-a-week job near her house. She did take a pay cut, but it was worth what she received in return: fewer hours and a job that was practically in her backyard.

We cannot eliminate nor halt the changes that are transforming the world of work. That is beyond our control. What we can control, however, is our response to the changes. Go ahead and experience the anger, if that is your initial reaction. Feel the frustration, delve into your sense of loss, and realize that anxiety comes with the territory. But then let go of it all. Understand that the new world of work is here to stay, at least for your lifetime; accept its limitations, and begin to focus on how you can take advantage of its opportunities.

Now's the time to switch from the big picture to your own personal snapshot of the situation. You can't control the world, the economy, your organization, your department, not even how your manager is handling the changes. You need to focus on creating a new view of yourself within the new world of work.

"Grant me the serenity to accept the things I cannot change, the courage to change the things I can, and the wisdom to know the difference."
Serenity prayer

Susan's wake-up call came when the high-tech medical-equipment company she worked for decided to merge with another company. She had already moved out of state and was telecommuting for the company, keeping it as her only client, but the merger would soon outplace her—in three months, to be exact. Her expertise was in marketing, so she began to devise a marketing plan for other medical-equipment companies in her area. With this new list of clients, she felt confident in her ability to respond to any new changes in the world of work.

Creating a "New View" of Yourself

You have to control what you can, and if that is limited to your own personal situation, then that is where you need to start. We're in the business of providing *"career makeovers"* for individuals. Don't mistakenly think that we're interested in coaching people only to look different. That never works for very long. Our strategy isn't to advise you to buy a briefcase, write a super resume, and go after every company that somehow resembles the one you currently work for.

Our success, and yours, is measured in the degree to which you change your mind set—in other words, we start with an internal makeover. Why? Because you can't look and act differently unless you think differently. Experience has taught us that achievement in the new world of work is realized only when you begin to view yourself as a independent contractor.

Becoming an independent contractor

Most people jump in here with, *"I know what an independent contractor is. It's someone who works for himself. I don't want to work for myself, so what does this have to do with me?"* Give us a minute, please. We want you to think of yourself as if you were an independent contractor, whether you work for yourself or someone else. You work for yourself, think for yourself, plan for yourself, and put yourself first. You, not your company, are in control of your life decisions.

Most of those whom we advise will end up working for someone else—their *"client"*— and there's no one saying you can't have one client for the rest of your life. What's important is that you view your work relationship in this new way. As an independent contractor, you continually need to prove yourself to your client. Conversely, you always need to be ready to go when the relationship doesn't serve both parties. It's a whole new way of behaving.

Consider how differently you would react when your company goes through a downsizing if you view yourself as an independent contractor. First of all, you'd probably already be aware of whether or not your job was truly adding value to the company. And second, your ties to the company would be less strong, thus lowering your *"give a rip"* level. You would already be marketing yourself to other clients.

Those who work for themselves know what we're talking about. You can't assume that longevity or perfect attendance will save you from some inevitable downsizing. You need to think of yourself as a small business that needs to be *"packaged"* and continually sold. People need to know who you are, what you do, and how you add to the bottom line.

Renewing your contract

This new mind set requires that you focus on the *"contract"* between you and your client(s) as an independent contractor would. Think of your annual review as a partial review of your contract, unwritten though it is. A review lets you know how your organization thinks you're doing. On your own, go a step beyond the review. Ask yourself:

♦ What have I accomplished this year?

♦ What do I want to accomplish next year?

♦ Am I being paid for the amount of time, effort, and expertise that I am contributing?

♦ Have I done some labor market research so that I know I am being paid fairly?

♦ Is it taxing my personal life too much?

♦ Am I bored, happy, challenged, etc.?

♦ Is there another way to contribute to this organization?

♦ Am I content to stay here?

When you are working for yourself, these questions are all valid and applicable. An independent contractor continually reevaluates his or her clients, and vice versa. You alone are responsible for your welfare and happiness. If you do not provide value to an organization, it is that organization's responsibility to let you go. If an organization doesn't meet your needs, it's up to you to leave. Responsibility is equally shared in the new world of work.

"You draw nothing out of the bank of life except what you deposit in it."
Anonymous

> *One of our clients, Maya Reynolds, questioned her contract on the fifteenth anniversary of her employment as head of training for a major bank. Having worked seventy or eighty hours a week during those years, Maya determined that her contract wasn't serving her well at all. She left the bank and came back as a consultant, and made them her first client. They were her first and only client for a year. Now the bank's work is only one-quarter of Maya's total business. Her anniversary questions made her rethink the value of her career.*

Loyalty is a non-issue

This new thinking requires an adjustment. It used to be that organizations took care of us. They supplied our medical, dental, and retirement benefits; they established co-ops and credit unions; and they handed out perks, such as trips, bonuses, parties, and fruitcakes at Christmas. It's usually at this point in our explanation that some individual raises his or her hand and asks, *"But I've been loyal to my company. Why haven't they been loyal back?"*

Loyalty hasn't gone away nor has it disappeared. It never existed. When the United States owned the world marketplace, companies desired for employees to stay from entry level to retirement. They took care of their employees' needs, acting like a paternalistic figure by supplying insurance and goodies to entice workers and then to keep them complacent. But an organization is a thing. It has no ability to be loyal. Policies, programs, and procedures only give the impression of loyalty.

So when individuals ask the loyalty question, we give them a litmus test for loyalty. We ask: *"Do you mean that you worked really hard? That you went the extra mile? That you gave up personal and family time?"* They nod their heads. *"But now comes the real test,"* we say. *"Did you in the course of your employment here turn down two better job offers to stay?"* That usually stops them in their tracks. Most likely, they never had their loyalty tested.

Whether or not you're an actual independent contractor, thinking like one will increase your success. Lincoln Electric, a company that builds welding equipment in Lincoln, Nebraska, is an example of an incredibly profitable company that treats its employees as independent contractors. Employees set their own schedule and are compensated according to their output. No benefits are provided, and employees are free to leave whenever they so desire. Not all jobs lend themselves to such an arrangement, but an *"independent-contractor"* mind set is still a critical indicator of career success.

Succeeding as an Independent Contractor

Career makeovers don't take place overnight, because a new mind set calls for commitment, time, and energy. To actually succeed as an independent contractor, you'll need to follow four steps:

1. Learn about the new world of work

2. Learn about yourself

3. Develop self-marketing skills

4. Do labor market research

Learn about the new world of work

"Find what you love to do, and you'll never work another day in your life."
Anonymous

You already have learned about the new world of work in chapters two and three of this book. On its own, this metamorphosis can be quite depressing. Unless, that is, you know how to translate the changes into a new pattern of behavior—that of the independent contractor. Changing your behavior occurs by following the next three steps, all of which are described in greater detail in the second half of this book.

Learn about yourself

What do you want to be when you grow up? Do you even want to grow up? These questions and more will be answered in this step. Many people make a career choice in their late teens or twenties and never swerve from that decision. We're here to challenge the notion that your first choice *(or your second or third)* is the best for you. Learning about yourself helps you pinpoint what you want from your career, and it enables you to make good decisions, see opportunities when they're in front of you, and create what others may consider lucky breaks.

> "It is better to be prepared for an opportunity and not to have one than to have an opportunity and not be prepared."
> Whitney Young Jr.

Develop self-marketing skills

This is an action step. Once you know where the work world is headed and you have determined where you want to go, developing marketing skills will help you realize your goals. It's not enough to know what you want; you have to be able to convince someone else that you can do it. Many people will spend a tremendous amount of time figuring out what really excites them, but are unable to communicate that excitement to anyone else.

> *Sarah, an information systems specialist, was laid off at a major food company and was placed in a displaced workers' pool with a year's time line to find a new job. In that year, Sarah took a temporary assignment in human resources, got a certificate in human resources, and applied for a job within the company in human resources. She was up against fifty other internal applicants, and she got the job. Ninety percent of the employees in the displaced workers' pool were let go, but Sarah's self-marketing skills got her the job she wanted.*

Do labor market research

Doing labor market research is another critical step, because the labor market is always changing. The names change, industries are continually growing and declining, and new jobs are being created all the time. You'll be researching what is happening within the labor market in which you want to live and work. You can't do it by reading national magazines or newspapers or the newest government publication. It is a personal process that needs to be done by you on a continual basis.

If you work for a large organization and you'd like to remain an employee of that organization, you can consider it your labor market. Much that you aren't aware of can take place in a large organization. You just may happen upon something that fits what you're looking for through research and talking to a variety of your fellow employees.

One of our clients, Tina Forsythe, worked in training at a major aerospace corporation. When the organization decided to move the training function to a different building, Tina volunteered to set up the facilities for the training department. She had to meet with the different vendors, including carpeting and office-furniture vendors, and she got to try her hand at space planning—deciding where the cubicles were to be placed, etc. She loved the experience so much, she talked to the facility planners within her corporation and found out about the career. Her labor market research resulted in her enrolling in the facility-management certificate course at the local university. When an opening came up in facility management at her corporation, Tina was regarded as an internal candidate and was hired over everyone else.

Independent contractors have the edge over other employees, because they are knowledgeable about the new world of work and about themselves, they have developed self-marketing skills, and they continually do labor market research. It's a plan for success that we have seen work time and time again.

Summary

The new world of work is a reality that elicits different feelings from different individuals. Whether you're angry or thrilled over the changes happening on the business scene, you have to realize that your response is the only thing about the changes you can control. Those who want to succeed in the new world of work will have to change their mind set, from that of a loyal employee to one of an independent contractor, whether or not they work for themselves.

Viewing a work relationship in terms of client and contractor takes the burden off of either party and places both in a position of proving value. If you want to succeed as an independent contractor, you will need to learn about the new world of work and yourself. In addition, you'll need to learn effective self-marketing skills and continually apply yourself to labor market research. It's a strategy that will definitely pay off—financially, psychologically, or both.

OFFICE CLOWN — RECEPTIONIST
FILE CLERK — ACCOUNTANT
SECRETARY — SECURITY
JANITOR — PRESIDENT

WHEN YOU'RE SELF EMPLOYED YOU WEAR MANY HATS

© 1992, 1994 HENRY MARTIN

Chapter 5 Key Points

🔑 Knowing yourself is the only way you can unlock the door to your career potential

🔑 Most people aren't in touch with their true desires, skills, and attitudes toward work

🔑 The keys to unlocking your career potential involve the following five areas:

- ◆ Attitude and motivation

- ◆ Work environment

- ◆ People, data, or things you wish to work with

- ◆ Skills

- ◆ Compensation

Try Unlocking Your Career Potential

5

We hate to break it to you, but we can't tell you which road to take on the path to career happiness, and anybody who professes to have a crystal career ball shouldn't be trusted. Why? Because only you can truly tell what interests you, how developed your skills are, and which of your needs must be fulfilled. You alone can discover the keys to unlocking your career potential. In our career consulting business, we have helped many individuals discover career happiness, but it didn't happen until they delved within themselves to uncover their true wants and desires. We provided direction and company, but they still had to walk down the path.

Once you know yourself, you will have the keys to unlocking your career potential. Analyzing yourself will provide you with a career checklist, much like a checklist you have when you buy a house or a car, when you date, or when you choose a college. It lists your priorities and simultaneously keeps you grounded in reality. You may wish to attend an Ivy League school, but your SAT scores direct you elsewhere, so you look closely at your other priorities.

To create your checklist, you must carefully analyze five different areas that relate to your life and your career choices. Then, once you've looked within, you will have the option of using the keys to unlock your career potential. To fully understand yourself and to tap into that career potential, you will need to examine the following five areas:

♦ Attitudes toward and motivation for work

♦ Environment in which you wish to work

♦ Desire for working with people, data, and/or things

♦ The skills you possess

♦ Your monetary expectations

"We will discover the nature of our particular genius when we stop trying to conform to our own or to other peoples' models, learn to be ourselves, and allow our natural channel to open."
Shakti Gawain

Why Do You Work As You Do?

Understanding your attitudes about work and your motivation for working is the first key to unlocking your career potential. Why do you want to work? Is it because you enjoy it, or because it pays the mortgage? Does the thought of work thrill you, or do you live primarily for the weekend? Our attitudes about work vary with our life experiences, and it's those same attitudes that color our motivation for working.

Where do our attitudes come from?

Our attitudes toward work are learned early on in life, in much the same way we develop our attitudes toward food and people. What we saw modeled in our own homes and exhibited by teachers or peers or the media set the groundwork for our own attitudes about work. Our attitudes develop from watching those around us work and listening to them talk about work.

> *A participant in one of our workshops specifically recalled how he developed a particular attitude toward work from what he saw at home. "You've heard the term 'nouveau riche,'" he said. "Well, my family was 'nouveau poore.'" He was from a long line of very wealthy people. The last person to earn much was his grandfather, who began to lose most of his wealth. "My father lost all of it," he remarked, "and we were the first generation of many who had to work. And none of us knew how, and none of us knew why, and I never saw any of it modeled in my home. Work was something only other people had to do."*

What did you first hear or observe about work?

_____

_____

_____

_____

_____

How motivated are you to work?

While your work attitudes remain fairly constant, your motivation for work changes as you enter different stages in the life cycle. The reasons why you work change as you marry, get unmarried, have children, have children leave home, take up a consuming hobby, experience a major illness or death in the family, get ready for a retirement career, or as you undergo any other major life transition. Why you work when you are fifteen is radically different from the reasons why you work when you're fifty.

Restaurant managers are well known for the many hours they contribute to work. Six-day work weeks and twelve-hour shifts are average. But we happen to know of one major restaurant chain that hires managers who want to make a good income and have a career, yet want adequate time to play. Most managers and workers attracted to this particular restaurant chain are either skiers or surfers, just like the founders, and the restaurants are located near either surf territory or the slopes. The restaurants are only open in the evening, so the managers have time to hit the surf or the slopes during the day and still pursue a career that can pay in the six figures.

What Do You Want to Get from Work?

Test your own reasons for wanting to work. Rank the following motivators from one to ten, with one being the most important motivator for you and ten, the least.

_____ Challenge

_____ Creativity

_____ Independence

_____ Influence over people

_____ Intellectual stimulation

_____ Monetary rewards

_____ Recognition

_____ Self-identity

_____ Serve people

_____ Social contact

"Motivation is what gets you started. Habit is what keeps you going."
Jim Ryun

Are you currently getting your top five motivators from the career or job you're in? If not, do you need to make a change to get them? If these motivators are important to you, and you are not getting many of your top five on a consistent basis, continue on the path to unlocking your career potential.

Where Do You Belong?

> "Some people could work in a cave if it were dry enough and light enough."
>
> Anonymous

The second key concerns work environment. Deciding where you belong holds great interest for some people and little interest for others. One of our clients, a human-resource professional, stipulated that she would only be happy working at a hotel or resort. Another client, a computer technician, told us that it didn't matter whether he worked for an aerospace corporation or a flower shop; in a tall, glass building or in a one-room shed; in a formal, multi-level corporation or a loose, informal company, as long as he was able to work with what he loved—computers.

A work environment is both a tangible set of physical assets and an intangible way of behaving. The tangible set includes such items as arena, industry, and size. The intangible way of behaving refers to organizational culture. If you have a distinct preference for a certain environment, then it is in your best interest to determine exactly what it consists of.

An arena is the largest description within the work environment. It involves the following sectors: business, nonprofit, education, and government. Which are you interested in? Do any of them not appeal to you?

> *Gayle Stoll, a woman we met at one of our workshops, was a high-school English teacher who made a career change from education to business. Attracted to the money and prestige of the entertainment industry, she went to work for a major television network, watching all of their shows in order to write promotional lead-ins for them. The environment was glamorous, and the money was good—she made $60,000 a year. However, she wasn't entirely happy in that setting.*

She thought carefully about one of the comments we made during our workshop—"The clues to your future are in your past"—and she started digging up old pictures. She discovered one that revealed her and other neighborhood children picketing for equal allowance. Not long after, she went to work for the ACLU in public relations and now is extremely content. She traveled from the education arena to business to nonprofit before finally finding her niche.

Industries

Once you've chosen your arenas, you need to look at the type of industries you are attracted to. Beside each industry listed, write down the first thought that comes to mind. It might be as generic as *"exciting"* or as specific as an actual company that the industry brings to mind. Then, circle any of the industries that you are strongly interested in or attracted to. Cross out with a line any that you wish to avoid.

_____ Aesthetic, Cultural

_____ Biomedical or Biotechnical

_____ Business/Corporate

_____ Computer

_____ Design

_____ Entertainment/Media/Broadcasting

_____ Fashion/Image

_____ Financial

_____ Governmental

_____ Healthcare/Nutrition/Fitness

_____ Hospital/Medical

_____ Hotel/Leisure/Recreation

_____ High Technology

_____ Food

_____ Educational

_____ Political

_____ Real Estate/Development

_____ Construction

_____ Retail

_____ Restaurant

_____ Telecommunications

_____ Consumer Goods

_____ Textile

_____ Manufacturing

_____ Sports/Leisure

_____ Travel/Transportation

_____ Utilities/Energy

_____ Consulting

_____ Computer Graphics

_____ Home-based Business

_____ Small Business/Franchise

Next, consider the size of the organization you'd like to work for. Size is critical to some people. Do you desire a small, young organization where you can play many roles and have an impact on the direction and development of a group? Or do you prefer a larger, older organization that has direction, stability, history, and prestige? Such an organization also can provide you with many avenues of growth simply because of size.

Choosing arenas, industries, and size are the tangibles within a work environment. Once you've chosen them, you're ready to look at the intangibles—the organizational culture that dictates how those in the organization behave. This is not information you'll find in the annual report.

What you will discover in determining an organization's culture is both the formal structure of the organization and the informal norms and values. Think about what environment you'd like in terms of how the people behave, communicate, look, and work together. Do you prefer an environment that is tightly structured and has a formal chain of command, or would you function better in a looser, more entrepreneurial environment?

> "For some individuals, a small company cuts off their circulation. For others, a large one is too impersonal. Find a size that fits you."
> Keith Stringfellow

> *Jack Browning, one of our clients who was an accountant, expressed a great deal of interest in motorcycles. He liked to be around them so much, he went to work for a major motorcycle distributor. Half of the employees rode motorcycles to work, including some of the secretaries. A real motorcycle was on display in the lobby, the walls were covered with pictures of motorcycles, and at lunch time, all the employees talked about...? You guessed it—motorcycles! Jack could have been an accountant anywhere, but he chose an environment that really interested him, and it increased his satisfaction.*

If a particular environment interests you, you will have a good starting point from which to direct your career inquiries. If you don't have much of an opinion one way or the other, your pool of possibilities will be much larger. It's unquestionably an individual choice that leads to a clearer definition of your ideal career.

With Whom Would You Like to Work?

Whom or what you work with is the essence of the third key to unlocking your career potential. Are you into people, data, or things? You would think that people would know intuitively with what or whom they prefer to work, but we've found that it's often the last thing on their minds. We've seen a number of data people in customer-service positions. They are terribly unhappy, but not sure why. Such a mismatch—between what or whom you want to work with and the reality of the position you're in—usually causes what we call *"career pain."*

Are you suffering from career pain?

"Realizing that a huge rift exists between your desires and reality can be incredibly unsettling. Try to build a bridge while you can still see the other side."
Denna Tredo

If you absolutely love your job, you most likely fit well in your position. But if you got laid off tomorrow, would you be able to describe exactly what type of job would fit your preference for things, data, or people? Most people cannot. And many people are not totally happy in their current positions (*i.e., they're suffering from some degree of career pain*), because perhaps they favor working with people while their work requires fixing things or playing with data. Or they would rather be by themselves, but they ended up in a career that involves a great deal of people contact.

Take a look at the following assessment. For each of the ten statements, check yes or no.

People, Data, Things—Which am I Into?

Yes___ No ___   1. I need to leave my work space often to get my *"people fix"* during the day.

Yes___ No ___   2. I love to be immersed in data.

Yes___ No ___   3. I've been fixing and tinkering with things since childhood.

Yes___ No ___   4. Interaction with people often leaves me energized.

Yes___ No ___   5. I'd rather gather the data and write the report than deliver the information to people.

Yes___ No ___   6. I get so caught up in working with data that I forget to eat.

Yes___ No ___   7. I love working with my hands.

Yes___ No ___   8. I feel challenged by working with groups of people.

Yes___ No ___   9. I would be very happy to work all day long by myself.

Yes___ No ___   10. I'm the first one to volunteer to head a committee or organize a meeting.

Scoring Key

"People" person: Answers yes to numbers 1, 4, 8, and 10, and no on number 9

"Data" person: Answers yes to numbers 2, 5, 6, and 9

"Things" person: Answers yes to numbers 3, 7, and 9

If there is a discrepancy between what you'd prefer and what your current job entails, you're probably suffering from career pain. Consider how you could alleviate it. Is it possible to expand or limit your *"people," "data,"* or *"things"* time to match your preferences? Or might a new position in a different organization be better? If a career change isn't in the cards, you can re-balance your life by emphasizing your preferences in your personal life. Introverts who are in people-oriented jobs often spend their weekends and vacations alone. And we've counseled extroverted clients who work in jobs with minimal people contact to do the opposite. They might join a bowling league or organize the PTA.

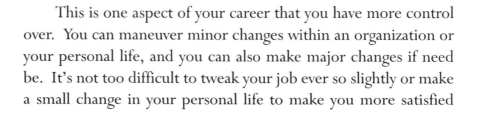

Rob Matthews, a client of ours, had a college degree, but he didn't know what he wanted to do. He happened upon the construction business, and he took a job in construction, which was basically a "things" job. While Rob was good with his hands, it wasn't satisfying to him. Eventually, he was promoted to a management position in the construction business, but he didn't enjoy managing people either. When we worked with him on assessing his preferences, we discovered that he liked a perfect combination of data, people, and things, each taking an equal third of his ideal work-day pie. He found a position within the financial world, where his work day is split equally between clients, the data they provide him with, and working on his computer. He could make more money if he had more clients, but he would never do that, because it would upset his preferred balance.

This is one aspect of your career that you have more control over. You can maneuver minor changes within an organization or your personal life, and you can also make major changes if need be. It's not too difficult to tweak your job ever so slightly or make a small change in your personal life to make you more satisfied with what or whom you work. Consider the following suggestions if you're interested in making minor changes:

♦ To increase your people contact, volunteer at work to participate on a committee or team.

♦ Talk to your boss about changing a task in your job description that you dislike.

♦ Conversely, talk to your boss about adding tasks that you enjoy.

♦ Balance your need for people, data, and things by pursuing a hobby or volunteer work that fills your need.

> *One of our clients, Myra Robinson, is vice president of information systems at a financial institution, which is a heavily data- and things-oriented job. Because she is such an extrovert, on her own time she serves on boards. She is on the Board of Directors at a local hospital, and she recently formed an advisory committee on women's health issues. Her volunteer work fills her need for people contact; participating in the volunteer work allows her to function well in a data- and things-oriented job.*

If you're considering a major change, please think it through carefully. Since any major change should take all five keys into consideration, you'll need to finish this chapter and chapter seven (*"Consider Making A Career Transition"*) before you hand in your resignation or approach your boss. But it is helpful to think about some of the options available to you if you can't be satisfied by making minor changes.

You may need to make a complete change in both your choice of career and the type of people you are working with. But before going to such an extreme, analyze why you are unhappy. Maybe your career is right for you, but you need to change the population of people you work with. One of our clients, Caroline Roshman, was a second-grade teacher who no longer wanted to teach second grade. She ended up going to graduate school, volunteered to teach an evening class of adult students, and discovered she loved it. She toyed with the idea of giving up teaching altogether, but now she's so glad she didn't, because she has found that teaching adults fits her fine.

Another change you might consider is doing something different with the same people. Jim Markworth, a manager of customer-service representatives at a major utility company, was tired of the long hours and the headaches involved in playing the manager role. He switched over to training the reps instead of managing them and is much more content.

Checking your balance of people, data, and things in your current position and determining if it fits your preferences is well worth your effort. For many, it's a connection they've never before made, one that makes a great deal of sense. And it brings you a step closer to unlocking your career potential.

What Do You Bring to the Table?

"Everyone has skills. You can't make it through life without mastering at least a few skills."
Anonymous

The fourth key to unlocking your career potential—pinpointing your skills—will open up doors to new career opportunities. We're willing to wager that you possess more skills than you believe you do, some which you developed outside the work arena and which could land you a job you would enjoy. And we also bet that you may be using some skills in your current job that you're not particularly thrilled about using.

Don't wait for the eulogy

Everyone is aware that they possess skills, and they can identify some of them. A participant in one of our workshops, Maurice Solvick, a real estate agent, told us he was good at sales. *"I know I am because I'm one of the top sellers, and I receive an award every year. But,"* Maurice said and paused to think for a moment, *"I can't really say that I'm good at much else. And while it provides a decent living, selling real estate is not my favorite activity."*

Unfortunately, like Maurice, most people don't come close to knowing all of the skills they possess. People often skate by for years without touching on everything that they do well, because they know they have some skills and that's sufficient for them. Yet awareness of your skills will help you unlock your career potential.

One of our clients, Margaret Trilling, a registered nurse who had been out of the work force for twenty years, came to us for career counseling. We asked her what skills she had, and she replied, "None." We investigated further, asking her what she did with her time. It so happened that Margaret's husband was a pilot who was shot down during the Vietnam war, and she helped start the MIA/POW group that eventually grew into a movement. She got together with other wives, and Margaret in particular decided the issue should receive national attention. She researched other major movements to learn about organization, and decided to go to Washington D.C. as an unpaid lobbyist. She was even brought into briefings with Henry Kissinger and Alexander Haig, took a world tour and met with heads of state and the Pope, and ended up in North Vietnam. She now works for her county in an advocacy position, lobbying for low-cost housing. This is our most extreme example of a client being unaware of the valuable skills she possessed.

It's at the end of our lives when people are willing to remember us for what we did well. But why wait for the eulogy? You need to know what you do well now, when you can choose to use those skills in a career that will satisfy you.

Pinpoint your skills

A skill is defined as *"a learned power of doing something competently."* The fact that it is a power implies that it affords you control. The more skills you possess, the more control you can have over your career. Don't get depressed here. When we explain this in our workshops, some of our clients start frowning and dropping their heads. When we ask them why, they respond with, *"But I don't have many skills. How am I ever supposed to get ahead?"*

Our response? *"You have many, many more skills than you think you do. Just wait. We're going to let you in on the three kinds of skills, and we'll ask you to identify each of those skills. If you don't list more skills than you thought you possessed, then you can get depressed."* But we guarantee you won't.

The three kinds of skills we describe to our clients are technical, personal, and transferable skills. Everyone possesses all three types of skills, although a few people rely solely on personal and transferable skills.

Technical Skills

Technical skills are specialized, job-specific skills that usually require training to learn. Such skills are obvious, measurable, and easy to describe. Typing, computer, accounting, lab research, sewing, engineering, and medical skills are all examples of technical skills. Most technical skills have to be kept up-to-date. Outdated computer or medical skills won't do you much good.

Besides technical skills, people also gather specialized knowledge. Specialized knowledge is a body of knowledge or information that you have accumulated over a period of time by learning about or working in a particular industry. It may be knowledge of labor law, how the legal system works, learning theory, personnel policies, wage and compensation procedures, how the body works, nutrition, etc. This body of knowledge is a marketable commodity, and is as important as the technical skills you possess.

> *Karen Elmwood, a special-education teacher who attended one of our workshops, recounted an example of how she acquired specialized knowledge that could have led to a new career. At the beginning of the school year, she was given ten children, and none of them were toilet trained. "I anticipated a very long year," Karen said. She hired a consultant who specialized in toilet training, and all ten children were trained within four months. The consultant offered Karen a position in her toilet-training practice, but Karen declined. "I knew more about toilet training than I wanted to know," she said. "I never thought about it being a marketable body of knowledge, but it was. I just wasn't interested in pursuing a career based on it."*

List any technical skills you possess. Put a star (★) by the skills you would like to continue to use in a work situation.

As with technical skills, you need to determine what knowledge you have and to what degree you want to continue using it. List your areas of specialized knowledge and put a star (★) by the knowledge you want to continue to use in a work situation.

_____   _____

_____   _____

_____   _____

_____   _____

_____   _____

_____   _____

_____   _____

_____   _____

Personal Skills

Some people think that skills only refer to specialized or technical abilities. Not so. Personal skills are skills that flow from personality traits and allow a person to adapt to various work roles and work conditions. We refer to personal skills as boy- and girl-scout qualities, such as integrity, perseverance, thoroughness, patience, commitment, and loyalty. They describe what you are like.

Personal Skills

Personal skills are traits or qualities that are useful in any career, any lifestyle, and life itself. Put a check (✔) by those personal skills you possess. Put a star (★) by the five (5) that you consider either your *"best"* or *"most important"* personal skills.

____ Hard-working	____ Flexible
____ Decisive	____ Fair
____ Independent	____ Helpful
____ Enthusiastic	____ Team player
____ Self-starting	____ Action-oriented
____ Creative	____ Empathetic
____ Personable	____ Forward-thinking
____ Goal-oriented	____ Humorous
____ Energetic	____ Clever
____ Friendly	____ Reliable
____ Eager	____ Punctual
____ Tenacious	____ Optimistic
____ Loyal	____ Cooperative
____ Trustworthy	____ Versatile
____ Quick-to-learn	____ Self-confident
____ Reasonable	____ Diplomatic
____ Thoughtful	____ Generous
____ Organized	____ Good judgment
____ Detail-oriented	____ Poised
____ Honest	____ Self-controlled
____ Meticulous	____ Tactful
____ Open-minded	____ Dependable

Transferable Skills

Transferable skills come from all areas of your life, and they never expire. Transferable skills are ones you use every day. They can appear at any age, and they go with you wherever you go. We describe them as a suitcase of valuable commodities that you take with you. You can go from the non-paid world of work into the paid world with this suitcase, from one industry to another, from job to job, or from one department to another.

What are some of these transferable skills? They range from communication, leadership, and management skills to program development, public relations, and promoting skills. Whether you're in a technical or a non-technical job, you will still use your transferable skills. For example, interpersonal and communication skills are important whether you are a teacher, computer programmer, manager, sales clerk, or doctor.

Transferable Skills

Look at the following list of transferable skills. Place a check (✓) by those you possess. Put a star (★) by those you enjoy using.

_____ Research and information-gathering	_____ Sales
_____ Communication	_____ Marketing
_____ Management	_____ Public Relations
_____ Leadership	_____ Teaching and Training
_____ Interpersonal	_____ Counseling
_____ Organizing and Implementing	_____ Analyzing
_____ Planning and Policy Development	_____ Problem Solving
_____ Creating and Developing	_____ Program Development
_____ Promoting	_____ Curriculum Development
	_____ Instructional Design

The technical, personal, and transferable skills you bring to a job are varied. Most likely, however, you are using skills you prefer not to use and not using skills you'd like to. How do you get around this dilemma? You pinpoint the skills you possess, and then determine which of those are your preferred skills. It's rewarding to analyze and reflect on the things you both do well and enjoy, because it provides you with exciting insights into what you should do to have a fulfilling career.

> *Melinda Schaefer, one of our clients who was a registered nurse, went to work for a large pharmaceutical company in customer service. She manages the employees who field questions from customers. By changing careers, Melinda wasn't able to use her technical nursing skills in her new field of work. However, she did take her personal and transferable skills with her. The transferable skills she acquired as a nurse— problem solving, communication, and interpersonal skills—helped her tremendously as a customer-service manager.*

Where Does Money Fit?

The fifth and final key to unlocking your career potential involves determining where money fits in your career picture. The issue of money is quite relevant to career decisions, because most people make career decisions with money in mind. Conventional wisdom uses money as a benchmark for success—*"You're only successful if you make a lot of money, and you can only be happy in your career if you make gobs of it."* Baloney. Some people feel that way, but you'll be extremely unhappy if you follow that road. More people place money in the middle of their career lists. They think it's important, but it doesn't take precedence over their desire to do something they enjoy.

> *One of our clients found himself in a dilemma. He got into sales because of the lure of a six-figure income, but it wasn't what he wanted to do. "I detest sales," he told us. "And the money doesn't help all that much. I spend it just to anesthetize my bad feelings about the job. I purchased a new home and a luxury car. And I go on expensive vacations to get away from my job. Now I'm stuck," he said. "I can't leave a job I hate, because I'll lose my house and my car. No other job I can get will pay enough to support my lifestyle."*

Your needs versus your wants

People continually confuse their wants and their needs; and, since most wants and needs are inextricably tied to money, it's an issue that must be addressed if you want to establish a healthier relationship with money. Most people think they need something that much more closely resembles a want. If you are considering a career or job change, you should get in touch with your true wants and needs.

All we have to do is ask people what they need, and they find it easy to list their desires. *"I need to make $100,000 a year,"* one person told us. *"I need to drive a Mercedes,"* said another. *"I need a 3,000 square foot home with an acre of land right next to the beach,"* says another. *"Hold on,"* we say. *"Your needs sound suspiciously like wants."* Are you in the habit of doing the same?

Needs are more general. They don't imply something quantifiable, nor do they refer to a particular label or status symbol. Fulfilling your needs means that you are satisfied, not ecstatic. While you may **want** to make $100,000 a year, your **need** is to be free from financial worries. That huge house is a want, while a home with a pleasant environment is a need. You may drool when you see a Mercedes, but you need to drive a vehicle that won't break down. Wants box you in; needs leave the options open.

"Money is the by-product—not the goal."
Randy Marsh

Look at the following list of examples. Then think carefully about your own needs and wants.

Needs	Wants
• Time for physical exercise • An appealing, comfortable, and safe home environment • Freedom from financial worries • New, stimulating surroundings • Time to be with my children • A good laugh at least once a day • Interesting work and mental stimulation • Time alone to pursue my art • Acceptance for who I am *(from me)*	• Membership in an exclusive gym • A 3,000 square-foot home by the beach • Earn at least $100,000 a year • An around-the-world trip • A vacation home in the desert • A trip to Disney World for the whole family • A promotion and more money • Art classes in Paris • My mother's approval

Fulfilling your needs is much easier than supplying your wants. And it just may be that you can fulfill all of your needs, even if you desire a job or career that pays less than your current one.

How do you get out of this mess?

Look carefully at what you spend your money on. If you have the desire to keep a diary of all your expenditures for a month or longer, by all means do so. It may be quite an eye-opener for you. If you'd rather not, try to be more aware of how you spend your money. A participant in one of our workshops discovered that he spent hundreds of dollars on magazine and newsletter subscriptions, many of which went unread. *"I've decided to stick with the one newsletter and two magazines I read. The others I can borrow from the library if I want to,"* he said. *"I've figured that this one change will save me two hundred dollars a year."*

We had one client who, until she paid attention to her finances, didn't realize that the low-fat muffin and gourmet cup of coffee she purchased every morning cost her twenty-five dollars a week. When she calculated the yearly charge—$1300—she nixed the muffins and brought a thermos of coffee from home. "The money I save will go toward paying off my credit card," she said. "And my goal is a balance of zero within eighteen months."

What's your current financial picture?

You may make $50,000 a year and not be further ahead of someone who makes $35,000. Why? Because the hidden cost of work may be more expensive for you. The $35,000 worker may not have to purchase high-priced work clothes, spend dollars in commuting every day, nor pay for child-care costs. It all depends on your job or career, and what you have to pay to work there.

How much does it cost you to go to work? Without knowing the true cost of going to your job, it is difficult to make future job or career decisions.

Brenda Weiss, one of our clients, made $32.50 an hour at her job, a job which required a long, daily commute. We explained the concept of determining your true hourly rate, and Brenda filled out the worksheet. After she threw in all her hidden costs—child care, car and commuting expenses, home maintenance, food, clothes, etc., she discovered that she made only $9.50 an hour. Brenda decided to open a home-based business. She takes care of her own kids, is free from her long commute, and makes $20 an hour after expenses, which is quite a bit more than her $32.50-an-hour job.

Freedom at last

We believe that the greatest gift you can give to your children or yourself is the ability to *"live below your means"*—to not spend all the money you make. Most people are searching for ways to live within their means, because they always end up living above their means. If you analyze your needs and wants, and consider all of your purchases before you make them, you may be able to live below your means. And just think of the career freedom you will have if you consistently *"live below your means."*

> *We conducted a career counseling workshop at a major organization that was downsizing. The room was packed with engineers who knew their days were numbered, and they were nervous, depressed, and full of anxiety. All except for one, a man by the name of Tim Hart. We asked Tim why he wasn't visibly upset. Tim told us that he had no debts, not even a mortgage. "I'm not worried about losing my job," Tim said. "I could get a job at a fast-food restaurant if I wanted, or not even work at all, because I don't need to make money." When we asked Tim how he did it, he said that he never increased his spending. "If I got a raise, I paid extra payments to my mortgage company. The same with my bonuses. I didn't find it that difficult to do."*

The issue of money is a loaded one, full of preconceptions and complexities. If you can focus on your relationship with money and understand what it can and can't do for you, you will begin to treat money in a healthy manner. Maintaining a healthy relationship with money involves analyzing your needs and wants, coming to grips with what your true hourly rate is, and determining whether you can live below your means. If you're willing and able to do all this, you may be on your way to financial independence and a whole new world of career opportunities.

"Keep your chin up. It's often the last key in the bunch that opens the lock."
Anonymous

Opening the Door to Career Options, Opportunities, and Choices

We've given you a lot to think about. But, by now, you should be much clearer about what you want from a career, what you have to offer, and how you can adjust your finances to accommodate your preferences. In this section, you'll pull all the insights you've uncovered into one succinct checklist.

You now have the keys in your hand. Some will be more important to you, based on your current desires; others may become critical at other stages in your life. That's the benefit of having these exercises. You can refer back to them at any time. Many of our clients tell us that they look over their career notebooks time and again.

Create your career checklist

Your career checklist is not set in stone. It's based on your motivations, desires, needs, and skills at this particular point in your life. Look over the checklist; then read through the example on page 70 written by a manager of technical support, Dan Moreno, age 37. In creating your own checklist, be as specific as you can, and as wordy as you'd like.

Career Checklist

Understanding Why You Work As You Do: Where does work fit into your life?

_____

_____

_____

Deciding Where You Belong: What or where is your ideal environment?

_____

_____

_____

Knowing Who To Work With: What is your ideal balance between people, data, and things? Who do you enjoy working with and in what way?

_____

_____

_____

Looking At What You Bring To The Table: What are your preferred skills?

_____

_____

_____

Determining Where Money Fits: Are you getting the financial reward you need or want? Are you headed toward financial independence?

_____

_____

Options:_____

Dan Moreno

Career Checklist

Understanding Why You Work As You Do: Where does work fit into your life?

I have always been very career oriented. I've been working since I was 14 and very rarely take a vacation. Work is still important to me, but I am ready for a change. I still need the challenge and creativity, but I don't want it to be so all-consuming. My kids are 8 and 10, and I really want to participate in their lives.

Deciding Where You Belong: What or where is your ideal environment?

I've always worked in large organizations. I have made good progress going through their ranks, but I am really tired of the bureaucracy and approval channels. I like the computer industry, but would like a smaller organization. I visited a small, international manufacturing firm last week, because I coach Little League with the owner. There were no private offices, and everyone was dressed in casual clothes and jeans. I don't know if I'm ready for such a big change, but I'm tired of this.

Knowing Who To Work With: What is your ideal balance between people, data, and things? Who do you enjoy working with and in what way?

I've always been very technically competent and "good with people." That's led me into supervisory and management positions. I've discovered that I can manage people, but I really don't want to. I don't mind leading a project, but I'd like to get out of day-to-day management. I also need to take a couple of technical classes to make sure I stay up-to-date.

Looking At What You Bring To The Table: What are your skills?

I have excellent interpersonal and communication skills. I'm highly organized and love to manage projects from beginning to end.

Determining Where Money Fits: Are you getting the financial reward you need or want? Are you headed toward financial independence?

If I leave this big organization and don't look for a management position, I need to anticipate some cut in income, at least for a while. In my experience, small organizations pay as well or better, but don't have such elaborate benefit packages. My wife and I are working on eliminating our short-term debt and reducing our long-term debt. I understand that the less debt I have, the more options I have. One of these days, I'd like to work for myself in a home-based business.

Options:

I'd like to do what I am doing now, either...
* *in a smaller organization as an individual contributor, but not as a manager, or*
* *as a subcontractor with several organizations as my clients.*

What do you do now?

Creating your career checklist won't do anything for you, unless you do something with it. If you have discovered through the exercises and activities in this chapter that you are perfectly happy where you are presently, then you can store the checklist, and fill it out at a later date when you feel ready for a change. You will have satisfied your urge to see if a change was necessary.

More likely, you have uncovered needs that aren't being met in your current position or preferred skills that aren't being utilized, or maybe you have discovered that a different environment would better complement your personality and work style. Whatever your career checklist reveals, you can either put it on the shelf or use it to your advantage. We suggest that you use it. And check out our book—*Unlocking Your Career Potential*. We provide many more exercises and ideas than can fit into this chapter.

"Purposeful action requires knowledge, insight, and the ability to 'get up and go.'"
Teri Burger

If you're in a state of *"analysis paralysis,"* and are having difficulty coming up with ideas of what to do, we give you the following suggestions:

♦ Look carefully at your checklist and note any ideas that pop into your mind. Many of our clients write little notes to themselves as they are going through their checklists, such as *"What about a position in marketing?"* or *"I'd be interested in telecommuting or working at home"* or *"Check out courses in computer literacy."* Doing so makes adding to the *"options"* part of your checklist much easier.

♦ Take a look at your own job and see where you can make changes. Many people find they only need to make minor adjustments to their own careers to be satisfied. One client negotiated a change in tasks—she dropped the writing of some detailed reports and took on some committee projects instead. Another client asked to move to a quieter cubicle. The change in environment made it easier for him to complete his work.

♦ Share your checklist with four or five people you trust and ask them for their suggestions. Sometimes you're too close to the issue to see what's obvious to others.

You own the keys that will unlock your career potential. Use them to open the door to new opportunities. Your career checklist will get you thinking about how you can work yourself into a job or career that's right for you. Swing that career door open. And, in the next chapter, you'll discover how you can market yourself to get that job or career you want.

Summary

You're at the end of the discovery process. What you have learned about yourself in this chapter you have captured in your career checklist. What have you discovered? Will you change nothing, tweak some specifics within your current position, switch to a different department, or head for a totally new career or job elsewhere? Choose what's best for you. And remember: whenever you feel that another change is in order, recheck the keys to unlocking your career potential. They'll work for the rest of your life.

"My eventual goal is to build a spaceship and colonize Venus, but for now I'm looking to move into a senior consultant position."

Chapter 6 Key Points

🗝 Marketing yourself is not bragging; instead, it's essential for anyone interested in career freedom and advancement.

🗝 If you're serious about self marketing, write and use bullet statements and create an *"I love me"* file

🗝 Realize that you're always in the right place at the right time to self market; you just need to take advantage of the opportunities all around you

🗝 Self-marketing scripts give you the power to effectively articulate your career desires

🗝 Promoting yourself within your organization means more than upward mobility; it also refers to lateral moves, moves down the ladder to take advantage of a different opportunity, and enriching your present job

Work on Marketing Yourself

6

You may have gotten along fine without self marketing. Some people never promote their own skills and accomplishments and are quite satisfied with their present jobs or careers. We're not saying that you can't get along without it in some circumstances. It's very possible that you can. We just want you to know that self marketing can take you much further than you thought possible. It can open doors to new opportunities. And it just may help you land the job or career of your dreams.

Doesn't It Sound Like Bragging?

In most cultures and most countries, parents raise their children to be humble, shy, and modest. One of parents' greatest fears is that their children will turn out to be braggarts. And no one likes a braggart. In the career workshops we conduct, we often ask our participants if their mothers ever sent them off to school with, *"Now you go to school and tell five people how wonderful you are today."* In the more than fifteen years we've been in business, not one person has answered *"yes."* More likely, you were raised with such sayings as:

◆ good work speaks for itself

◆ children should be seen and not heard

You bring such ideas to the marketplace. If you're not quite sure whether you're cut out for self marketing, you probably picked up on that attitude about self marketing from your parents and kept it for your own.

Consider the following: on an interview, who gets the offer—the best candidate or the best interviewee? The best interviewee, of course. The two may possibly be one and the same, but not necessarily. Whoever can talk about and present him or herself in the best manner will get the offer. When you're sitting in an interview, the interviewer is not going to consult with your mom, your teachers, your colleagues, or your former boss. It's strictly up to you to speak for yourself.

A company that was going through a major reorganization had to simultaneously lay off a large number of employees and redirect the others to new positions. Every department relinquished its employees, and the directors and vice presidents had to choose who would remain and what jobs they would hold. In a hotel room, the decision makers taped flip-chart pages listing all of the available positions around the perimeter of the room. Then, one by one, employees' names were called out and the directors had to answer "yes" or "no"—whether they wanted to keep that individual or not. One of the directors later

told us about the process. "We were literally playing musical chairs with people's livelihoods. Unfortunately," he said, "a lot of people who were very good at what they did were let go, simply because no one knew them. When their names were called, there was dead silence, and they were placed on the layoff list." Even the names of those who received a negative response were sometimes kept; a director who hadn't worked with them would opt to keep them, because at least they were known.

Self-promotion skills are survival skills. You will be working for many different people, whether as an employee or as an independent contractor, throughout your working years. Knowing how to market yourself and your career will help you keep your head above water and keep you paddling even when you're in the midst of a career storm.

Jump-Starting the Self-Marketing Process

In self marketing, the emphasis is on *you*. You are the product that needs to be packaged and sold, so you'll be working on how best to do that. Yes, eventually you will need to get out there and sell yourself; but, in order to do that successfully, you'll have to know yourself, your skills, and your accomplishments inside-out. For some of our clients, this part of the process is fairly simple and enjoyable; for others, it's like pulling teeth.

Whenever you present yourself formally *(e.g., in a job interview)* or informally *(e.g., in everyday conversation)*, you need to focus on the specifics of what you can do or what you've done.

"If you don't promote yourself, a terrible thing happens—nothing."
Anonymous

Most people talk in glittering generalities, such as:

♦ *"I'm good"*

♦ *"I'm great with people"*

♦ *"I'm a hard worker"*

♦ *"I've got a degree in <u>(fill in the blank)</u>"*

So what? Those phrases are not terrific self-marketing tools. Until you start to document your skills and accomplishments in the form of bullet statements *(we'll show you how soon)*, you're never going to impress anybody, get the job or promotion you want, or earn the money you think you deserve. Generalities make you sound like everybody else. They're flat, unimpressive, and ho-hum.

Bullet statements focus on what you've done and what you can do for others. Writing bullet statements means that you have to look back on the events of your life and pull meaningful accomplishments from them, accomplishments that market you successfully. Bullet statements succinctly describe the accomplishments and skills that you want to stand out.

Putting together an "I love me" file

To write effective bullet statements, you must remember your skills and accomplishments. However, the older you are and the more jobs you have held, the more difficult it is for you to remember all of them. That's why we ask our clients to create an *"I love me"* file. What is an *"I love me"* file, you ask? It's similar to the file of report cards, awards, and mementos your parents kept for you or which you are creating for your children. The *"I love me"* file is just an adult version.

"Words are a form of action, capable of influencing change."
Ingrid Bengis

What goes in your *"I love me"* file? So many different items that we suggest you clean your desk, clear out your closets, and go on a data search. You'll be looking for:

- copies of your resumes or job applications *(include **all** resumes, because different resumes will highlight different skills and accomplishments)*

- all old performance evaluations *(if you don't have them, your old employers will; you may have to pay for a copy, but it's worth it)*

- any letters of recommendation

- anything written about you *(were you written up in a company newsletter, featured in a volunteer newsletter, a magazine review, etc.?)*

- any awards or certificates you received, for either professional or volunteer work

- samples of your work

- letters from satisfied customers, students, trainees, etc.

- your bullet statements written on 3x5 cards *(every time you've had a major accomplishment that can be written as a bullet statement, do so and place in your file)*

You need to have a hard copy of all the items in your file. So if you have some of the items on disk or on the hard drive of your computer, make a copy and drop it in your file.

Your *"I love me"* file is invaluable. And you only have to update it once or twice a year. It's actually a great morale booster, and you can take it with you on an internal or external interview. It is by no means used on every interview, but should someone want a sample of something, it's worth a thousand words. It's your success portfolio.

> "The longer you can look back, the further you can look forward."
> Winston Churchill

> "Don't tell me how hard you work. Tell me how much you get done."
> James Ling

Hitting your target with bullet statements

Bullet statements are such short, action-oriented statements, they deter people from talking ad nauseam about themselves. If you're at the water cooler with a manager from another department or in a job interview with the personnel director from another company, you don't want to dawdle. You must get your point across quickly. Bullet statements are fast and sharp, and they hit their target.

Interviewers, bosses, and contact people want to know two things, and two things only: what you did and what happened as a result. If you want to list your tasks and responsibilities on your resume or recite them to current or prospective employers, you'd better be prepared to tell what resulted from those tasks and responsibilities. Too many people leave it at: *"I was responsible for the annual awards banquet."* Well? Did you have it? Did anyone come? And, if people did attend, what happened while they were there?

Learning to write bullet statements

Writing bullet statements is often trickier than it looks. We've found that our clients are most successful when they see how other people have written them and then practice writing bullet statements themselves. The following bullet statements should stimulate your thinking. Most of them are transferable to at least ten different careers or jobs.

1. Reduced costs and overhead expenses by careful monitoring and control of financial assistance and repayment procedures.

2. Conducted fifteen-hour training course for newly-recruited volunteers; increased effectiveness by 50 percent.

3. Founded a real estate partnership while in law school. Parlayed the original investment capital of $30,000 into over $500,000 in five years.

4. Was instrumental in founding the University of San Diego Business Association. Developed a program to create an awareness of and an interest in the business community.

5. Directed a team of eight professionals to assess needs, establish goals, and target objectives to meet the individual needs of a group of handicapped individuals.

Are you getting a better idea of what a bullet statement is? The people who wrote the preceding bullet statements identified a situation, the action they took, and the results they achieved. Once you've come up with these three categories, your bullet statements will be easier to write.

First, you'll list the SITUATION. You'll need to state the situation or problem that confronted you. Try to be as detailed and specific as possible.

Second, you'll describe the ACTION you took. You will have to recall what you did to solve the problem. Use an action verb, or more than one action verb, if appropriate.

Third, you'll report the RESULTS. Your objective is to tell what the outcome was of the action you took. Quantify, if possible, and use percentages and estimates.

You'll be writing your bullet statements in two drafts. The first draft will contain jargon and work content. As you write the second draft, be conscious of words that aren't transferable. For example, use *"organization"* instead of *"school,"* and use *"client"* or *"participant"* instead of *"student"* or *"patient."*

Finally, when you've finished your second draft of Situation-Action-Results, you will formulate a short, concise statement that communicates your skill. This will be your final bullet statement, and you should be able to use it in any conversation.

Look at the following example. Then we'll give you a chance to try your hand at writing one.

SITUATION: *I needed to write the marketing plan for the largest market in our company.*

ACTION: *Gathered objectives and plans from each area, compiled, and then wrote my own section.*

RESULTS: *All marketing department personnel were clear on goals, and management had one document to track the objectives through the year.*

BULLET STATEMENT: *Gathered and compiled objectives and plans from each department to create a marketing plan for the Los Angeles/Orange area. All marketing department personnel were clear on goals, and management had one document to track the objectives through the year.*

Now it's time for you to write one of your own Situation-Action-Results and its corresponding bullet statement.

SITUATION/PROBLEM:

_____

_____

_____

ACTION/TASKS:

_____

_____

_____

RESULTS/CONSEQUENCES:

_____

_____

_____

BULLET STATEMENT:

_____

_____

_____

Bullet statements can be used in both informal and formal settings. Don't only include them in resumes or job interviews, also use them when talking to colleagues, in professional meetings with your peers, when conversing with your boss at the company picnic, and/or in the midst of a training class.

Monica Breyer, a participant in one of our workshops, called to tell us how she had received a job offer by self marketing in an informal setting. A special education teacher for the deaf and mentally handicapped, Monica, through our program, had identified that she wanted to be in training. While flying to a family emergency, she happened to strike up a conversation with her seat partner. "He asked me what I did, and I was prepared to answer thanks to your training," she told us. "I am a teacher and a trainer. I love to take complicated ideas and break them down into smaller parts. I take them to my students' level of learning and am thrilled when they grasp the previously unattainable concepts." Monica's seat partner was the owner of a national hamburger chain. He was extremely dissatisfied with his trainers, whom he thought trained too theoretically. He made Monica a job offer on the spot.

You have to begin your self-marketing process with a good look at yourself and what you can do. Then, and only then, can you begin to write bullet statements about your accomplishments that will hit your target audience—your boss, a prospective employer, or a new contact you made. Your bullet statements should be used continually, as well as be placed in your *"I love me"* file, which you will use whenever you want to write a winning resume or prepare for an interview or a performance evaluation. Doing these things will enable you to set the self-marketing process in motion.

"Your most important sale in life is to sell yourself to yourself."
Maxwell Maltz

Techniques and Strategies for Being in the Right Place at the Right Time

You're most likely aware of the saying, *"You need to be in the right place at the right time."* We've heard many clients moan over the fact that they were in the wrong place, or that their timing was off even though the place was right. We don't buy that. The fact is that you're always in the right place at the right time. You're just not taking advantage of it.

Cashing in on your current activities and contacts

Many people are unaware of the opportunities around them. They're so focused on their current jobs and problems that they can't see beyond the blinders they have on. So much of *"being in the right place at the right time"* is understanding that every place is the right place, and every time is the right time for self marketing. There's not just one time and one place in your lifetime that is your ticket to career success. If that were the case, career success would be as improbable as winning the lottery jackpot.

It's our premise that you must self market everywhere in order to get the word out about who you are, what you can do, and what you want. To get comfortable with this tactic, we have our clients make a list of all the places they frequent. Then, when they find themselves in those particular environments, it registers that they should start to self market.

Where do you hang out? Usually the places you find yourself in can be divided into two categories—your personal life and your professional life.

Personal Life

In the pursuit of personal activities, where do you go? To the neighborhood market or the closest strip mall? Look at the list that we have started for you, and add the places you visit on the lines that follow. They may prove to be valuable places for meeting new contacts who could help further your career.

I Can Contact People At...

Kids' soccer games

Church activities

Homeowner meetings

Orthodontist's waiting room

Gym

_____

_____

_____

_____

_____

_____

_____

_____

Professional Life

Now you'll make a list of where you could make contacts within your current organization. Think beyond the scope of your boss's office, and look for all the opportunities where you could self market.

I Can Self Market...

In the cafeteria

At a task-force meeting

In a volunteer committee

At a training class

In the elevator

Rick Endicott, a client of ours, was a teacher who did some teleconferencing for his school district. At a school fund-raiser, Rick decided to use his self-marketing skills. "Instead of telling people I was a teacher," he said, "I focused on the teleconferencing project I had just completed." One of his new contacts was a vice president at a large aerospace firm. "His firm was considering investing money in a teleconferencing center," Rick shared with us. "I gave him my business card, and he contacted me the following week. I met with the personnel director at his firm and was offered a job. I'm a living example of the power of self marketing."

Presenting Yourself in a Positive Manner

Self marketing is a breeze if you have skills and accomplishments to talk about, and you know how to look and sound good in the process. You've already analyzed your skills and accomplishments in order to determine which ones to feature, and you realize that you have to self market continually and everywhere you go. You've done a great deal *(but not all)* of the necessary work involved in self marketing. Now we're going to teach you how to create a self-marketing script that works for you. Then we're going to ask you to critique your image, and encourage you, if necessary, to upgrade it.

Using the power of words to gain a new image and visibility

"When you know where you're going, tell others. They might have directions for getting there."
Debbie Cahoon

You may be ready for a change—a new career, a promotion, or perhaps a different job within your organization. But have you made the necessary changes in how you talk about yourself? What you say about yourself—in introducing or talking about yourself—is so very critical to the self-marketing process. Many people have no idea of the power of the words that come out of their mouths. They're not even conscious of the fact that what they're saying or not saying is being judged.

A participant in one of our workshops found it difficult to conceive of promoting herself verbally. *"My boss can see that I stay late, and I know she notices when I work especially hard on a project. Why isn't that enough?"* Good question. But while words without actions to back them up won't make an outstanding impression, actions without words often get overlooked. Don't leave your career to chance. You need to learn to use the power of words to make yourself visible and steer your career in the right direction. You'll need to learn how to create your own self-marketing script.

"Actions speak louder than words only when someone is watching." Jeff Stingley

Creating your self-marketing script

Your self-marketing script, carefully prepared, will put you ahead of the game when introducing yourself in a networking group, responding to questions in a job interview, or when describing your skills to someone in a social situation. Your script will tell others that you are qualified and appropriate for your chosen career or position. It will show the match between what's required for the job you're after and your skills, experiences, and qualities.

It's much easier to market yourself and say your lines if you've thought of the lines beforehand and have practiced them. That's why we want you to understand what goes into a self-marketing script and why we want you to create your own and practice it.

Your self-marketing script will tell others:

1. where you are now, your past experiences, and what has made you special and successful in your current role

2. where you are going—your general or specific career goal

3. the skills and qualities you have to take with you

When we interview successful clients and ask them what was one of their most helpful self-marketing practices, they often state that it was the opportunity to start talking about themselves and presenting themselves before they were actually on the job interview. Their self-marketing scripts gave them the confidence to begin this. A job interview can be tension-producing, but if you've had practice presenting yourself and know your lines, it becomes less stressful and, perhaps, even fun.

Before you can do a good job of writing your marketing script and presenting yourself, you must think through your past skills, experiences, and knowledge to see which are related to your targeted career.

Your background statement

Your background statement is a brief summary of either your prior experience or your current job. It's just a way of letting people know where you've been or where you are. Use whatever is appropriate. If your current job is most reflective of your skills for the position you're after, use that. In some instances, it will be stronger to summarize other work experiences.

Where you're headed

In your self-marketing script, you also need to identify where you are going. Are you looking to expand what you currently do, find a similar position in a different industry, or totally change careers? Your listener can't help you unless you verbalize what you want.

Summary of your skills

What you'd like to leave your listener with is a summary of your skills. The person or the people you're talking to may be able to infer your skills by the other things you have said, but you never want to count on inferences to make your point. We counsel our clients to be very clear and even repetitive if they need to be.

For example, a teacher who wants a position in sales might say, *"In summary, I feel I bring communication, interpersonal, educational, and training skills to the field of sales. In addition, I'm motivated, I'm a self starter, and I'm quick to learn."*

In some situations you'll use a longer version of your self-marketing script; in others, a short one is what makes sense. That's why we've included a sample of each. Read through them to get a good feel for what's involved in a self-marketing script.

Longer script for interviews:

"I'm Bob Jones. My background includes conceptualizing and managing a preschool, and initiating and coordinating adolescent programs in psychiatric hospitals. The success of these programs was due in great part to my marketing and public relations activities. I'm in a career transition, focusing on public relations and/or community relations in the health field for an educational institution."

"Never bend your head; always hold it high. Look the world straight in the face."
Helen Keller

Shorter version for introductions at meetings:

"I'm Bob Jones. My background includes managing and promoting a preschool and adolescent programs in psychiatric hospitals. I'm in a career transition, focusing on public relations and/or community relations in the health field for an educational institution."

Upgrading your personal presentation

In addition to what you say about yourself, the image that you project greatly influences those around you. When you are confident about how you look and the image you portray, your personal effectiveness increases. Your personality and your self image are magnified by the way you look.

We run across many people who are resentful of or unhappy about the fact that their personal image makes such a difference. But it does. If *"dressing for success"* makes you uncomfortable, please realize that in some environments you won't go very far unless you do dress for success.

In most organizations, the higher you go, the dressier it gets. But it's up to you whether or not you want to join the *"dressing game."* If you don't want to move up the ladder in an organization that does play the dressing game, you don't have to. It's your choice.

Some of our clients go on and on about how phony the whole game is. Since we dress professionally when we conduct our workshops, if our clients protest too much about projecting a professional image, we stop them and say: *"Okay, you've formulated an impression about us in the time we've spent with you. We enjoy talking with you, and we can tell that you like the class. But what if we came into this room dressed in shorts? What would you have thought?"* This scenario stops most of them in their tracks. The fact is that they would be very disconcerted if we led our workshops dressed in shorts.

> *At a major corporation that was downsizing, a number of employees were told that they had three months to find a new position within the organization, or they would be outplaced. Most of these employees had worked in regional offices where the dress was informal, and they were brought to headquarters where the dress was much more formal. One employee recounted the difference in dress: "I was used to wearing jeans and cowboy boots at my office, and suddenly I was thrust into an environment of suits and ties. It was a shock to my system." Twenty-five of the thirty employees made the transition to formal dress and got jobs within the organization. The five who continued to dress exactly as they had prior to the downsizing lost their jobs.*

Looking good and saying the right things won't do everything for you, but they just may give you the push you need to get the promotion you want or the position you've been after. Don't disregard the power of the words that come out of your mouth or the power of the image you project. Create a self-marketing script that promotes you effectively, and that is also comfortable to recite. Then practice it and perform it. And remember to upgrade your image so that it fits the job you'd like to get.

Promoting Yourself within Your Own Organization

It could be that you're not interested in changing careers. Maybe you don't even want to switch industries or organizations. You really like the company you work for; your only gripe is that you don't want to stay in the same position doing the same things for the rest of your life. We hear such statements from our clients on a regular basis. Some already feel stuck; others just want

"The dictionary is the only place where success comes before work."
Arthur Brisbane

information for when they're ready to make a move in their organizations.

When we tell our clients that we're going to help them promote themselves within their own organizations, they immediately think we're talking about moving up the career ladder to a higher position. Certainly, many of our clients are interested in such a move, but that's a limited view of the whole promotion issue. We also see promotion as promoting yourself in the same position you're in now, promoting yourself laterally, or even promoting yourself to a new opportunity by moving down the ladder to regroup and see where you want to go next.

Making a lateral move

A lateral move is a good option to consider, because it can result in a win-win situation for both the employee and the organization. If you choose to make a lateral move, you get a new career, new challenges, new skills, new people to interact with, and you do not risk leaving your organization, which is a *"known"* to you. Your company also benefits. It gets a rejuvenated employee who is already socialized within the organizational culture.

Many of our clients have wisely chosen lateral moves. One young woman discovered through the career-assessment process that she wasn't cut out for her current position in customer service. *"I couldn't stand the constant contact with irate customers,"* she explained. *"So I bided my time until an opening came up in purchasing. It was a much better match for my skills. I applied, got it, and am happy I didn't leave the company."* Her story is one of many we hear from clients who made lateral moves and knew it was the right choice for them.

The realities of climbing the ladder

What if you're interested in climbing up in your organization? The messages you've heard from your parents, from school, and from society at large on the subject of climbing the corporate ladder are strikingly similar: *"Success is measured by how fast you climb it, and how close you get to the top."* Oh, sure, some parents say their only concern is that you're happy, but they certainly aren't thrilled with a lousy report card or a pink slip from your employer, no matter how happy you appear to be.

Before we get into the details of promoting yourself upward within your organization, we suggest you decide whether it's really what you want or need. In reality, climbing the corporate ladder is becoming more difficult as organizations are getting flatter. You need to determine your own definition of success. If that includes moving up, fine. If not, that's fine also.

Take the following quiz to get an idea of whether or not you'd be willing to work your way up the ladder.

"With your ability and your experience, in six months you could be pulling down three hundred thousand here as a junior partner, and there's no one to stop you but me."

Am I Cut Out for the Corporate Climb?

Check whether you agree or disagree with each of the following statements.

Agree____ Disagree ____   1. My personal life takes a minimum amount of my time.

Agree____ Disagree ____   2. I am willing to work more than a forty-hour week.

Agree____ Disagree ____   3. I want to work outside my job description.

Agree____ Disagree ____   4. I enjoy taking on new tasks and responsibilities.

Agree____ Disagree ____   5. I don't mind serving on task forces and committees and attending meetings.

Agree____ Disagree ____   6. I don't mind taking responsibility for other people's work.

Agree____ Disagree ____   7. I'm ready to be held accountable for more end results.

Agree____ Disagree ____   8. I tend to see and think in the big picture.

Agree____ Disagree ____   9. I'm ready for more interaction with customers, clients, and/or upper management.

Agree____ Disagree ____   10. I am comfortable in new situations and welcome change.

Agree____ Disagree ____   11. I enjoy working without direct supervision.

Agree____ Disagree ____   12. I can manage my own time and schedule.

Agree____ Disagree ____   13. I understand that I may be viewed differently by my colleagues and peers.

Agree____ Disagree ____   14. I constantly look for new educational and training opportunities, done on company time or my own personal time.

Agree____ Disagree ____   15. I am eager to contribute to my field through professional organizations.

Scoring Key

Count the number of times you checked *"agree."*

11-15: You most likely are ready for promotion and/or are already attempting the climb. Read through this chapter to learn how to maneuver the heights more easily.

6-10: Think through your reasons for wanting to climb the corporate ladder. You may decide to implement our ideas more slowly, choose a lateral move, or prepare to climb sometime in the future.

0-5: You're not ready at this time. Don't attempt the hike until you're comfortable with the realities involved and can put up with the pitfalls.

Working smart and getting where you want to be

Many people mistakenly think that a promotion means a totally new job with brand-new responsibilities. That's usually not the way it works. If you've been promoted, it's much more likely that you've already been handling many of the responsibilities that are attached to your new position or job title. You generally ease into a new position.

"This is good news," we tell our clients. Why? Because it means that you can often work your way into a promotion or a lateral move within your organization: or, you can gain skills to make a move outside your organization. But it requires that you work smart and take advantage of job enrichment.

"The real risk is doing nothing."
Denis Waitley &
Remi L. Witt

"Job enrichment?" you ask. *"Sounds like a fancy term. What is it?"* Well, it's actually a good description, because it refers to a conscious choice on your part to enrich your job. It means changing your present position to expand the scope, visibility, autonomy, challenge, attractiveness, meaningfulness, and/or learning potential of your job. We know that's a mouthful, but it's the only way to describe job enrichment that does it justice.

It's called job enrichment, because it differs from job enlargement in that **you** decide to change your job because **you** want to. You take the initiative to change your job, and you can change the quality as well as the quantity of tasks. Job enlargement is someone else's choice to increase the tasks you do. For example, let's say that you currently do tasks A, B, and C. Your boss comes to you and says, *"You're a busy person, but I think you can also handle tasks D, E, and F."* Congratulations! Your job has just been enlarged.

Job enrichment can include one or a combination of the following strategies:

1. Improving your present performance by identifying an area of weakness and deliberately working on that weakness. *(Example: If you're not really strong on a particular computer program, you opt to take a software class on company time or your own time.)*

2. Taking on a task, a project, or an event that you find enjoyable and that builds on a particular strength or skill. *(Example: After taking the software class, you're a whiz on the computer program, so you offer to teach the rest of your department.)*

3. Taking on a task, a project, or an event that allows you to learn and try an *"untried"* skill. *(Example: Perhaps your company is offering a course on public speaking; you decide to take it, because you have no experience in public speaking.)*

4. Taking on a task, a project, or an event that will allow you greater recognition and credibility within your organization. (*Example: Since your organization's big push this year is to work with the Girl Scouts, you decide to join the committee that will be the liaison between your organization and the Girl Scouts.*)

5. Asking for an opportunity to take total responsibility for a task, a project, or an event that you now do only a part of.

> One of our clients, Lani Glenn, was a medical technical writer for a major pharmaceutical company. She decided to use strategy #4— taking on a task, project, or event that would allow her greater recognition and credibility. Lani volunteered to be part of a committee that put on her organization's major annual conference for doctors. "For three years, I worked on the committee," Lani said, "and I kept up my technical writing work at the same time." She took on more and more responsibility every year. "Finally, I was ready for strategy #5—taking on total responsibility for a task, project, or event," Lani told us. "I went to my boss and said, 'If there's an opening, I would like to have the job that takes full responsibility for the major conference.' And I got it. I left my technical writing behind, and became the meeting planner for the conference."

Working your way up in your own organization can be done. First, however, it's critical that you determine if you really want to climb the corporate ladder. Not everyone is willing to pay the price. Some people decide to stay where they are, make a lateral move, or even choose realignment. Whatever your choice, begin to enrich your job in every possible way. Also, consider reading our book—*Marketing Yourself and Your Career*. It's packed full of additional activities, real-life stories, and tips on self marketing. And don't forget to read the next chapter. It's essential if you're considering a career move.

> *David Krosby, a participant in one of our workshops who worked for a major computer corporation, discovered through assessing his career that he was climbing the corporate ladder and didn't want to. Most companies "reward" employees by moving them up, giving them more work, a title, more responsibility for others' work, and higher pay. David told us, "I learned through your class that I thoroughly enjoyed technical work. I didn't enjoy supervising others who did the work I loved." David elected to go back to his original position (i.e., he chose realignment). And he's much happier.*

Summary

It's in your best interest to learn how to promote yourself. Get over the notion that your good work and good deeds will speak for themselves. You, and you alone, are responsible for letting others in the world of work know what you can do. Take advantage of this opportunity to learn how to do it well. It does take commitment, but once you learn how to self market, it will become a habit that you'll never want to break.

"I got the job"

© 1992, 1994 AL ROSS

Chapter 7 Key Points

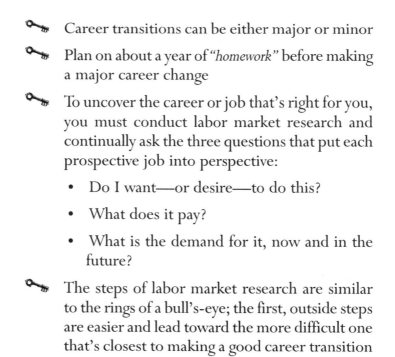

🔑 Career transitions can be either major or minor

🔑 Plan on about a year of *"homework"* before making a major career change

🔑 To uncover the career or job that's right for you, you must conduct labor market research and continually ask the three questions that put each prospective job into perspective:

- Do I want—or desire—to do this?

- What does it pay?

- What is the demand for it, now and in the future?

🔑 The steps of labor market research are similar to the rings of a bull's-eye; the first, outside steps are easier and lead toward the more difficult one that's closest to making a good career transition

Consider Making a Career Transition

7

In nearly every company, during the course of each day, someone considers making a career change—a fleeting thought of *"What if,"* a serious consideration that balances the pros and cons of a change, or even an edict from the powers-that-be to move on. Whether you're unhappy, bored, unfulfilled, or just plain given the shove, a career change may be in your cards. Don't disregard the possibility. It could prove to be one of the best moves you'll ever make. But do be forewarned—proper planning is essential for a successful career transition.

You Are Constantly in a Career Transition

You do need to be aware that major career transitions—transitions in which you completely change your field of work—take at least a year to accomplish. That's the average time schedule, and it's the case with just about any major change. A spouse doesn't leave a partner based on the whim of a particular moment. The seeds are often planted far in advance of the actual divorce. Likewise, a cross-country move. How many people do you know pack up their belongings and move without any forethought whatsoever?

However, some people suppress thoughts of a career change. When such thoughts enter their minds, they push them down into their subconscious. There's too much at stake, it's too risky, their spouses won't like it, it's too difficult, it will take too much time, etc. But their thoughts still work on them anyway. In time, they begin to see signs that they're ready for a career transition.

Picking up signs that point toward a career change

"It doesn't do any harm to dream as long as you get up and hustle when the alarm goes off."
Anonymous

We've seen it happen over and over again. Our clients would sometimes reveal different symptoms of career dissatisfaction, but they all noticed particular signs that pointed them toward a career change. What about you? Are you showing any early-warning signs? Take the following quiz to see if a career transition is in your near future.

Am I Experiencing Early-Warning Signs?

Agree_____ Disagree _____ 1. I start to feel anxious on Sunday afternoon, because I don't look forward to going to work on Monday morning.

Agree_____ Disagree _____ 2. I experience one or more chronic physical symptoms, such as headaches, stomach problems, and/or backaches.

Agree_____ Disagree _____ 3. On Sunday morning, I automatically reach for the funnies or the sports page, but then decide to check the want ads first.

Agree_____ Disagree _____ 4. At work, I find myself constantly watching the clock.

Agree_____ Disagree _____ 5. I feel like I'm on a treadmill that doesn't have an *"off"* button.

Agree_____ Disagree _____ 6. At a work meeting, I seem to be less excited than anyone else in the room.

Agree_____ Disagree _____ 7. I don't really care about any promotions at work.

Agree_____ Disagree _____ 8. My *"give-a-rip"* level is low.

Agree_____ Disagree _____ 9. I fantasize about doing something totally opposite from what I'm currently doing.

Agree_____ Disagree ___10. I've started counting the years, months, and/or days until retirement.

How many of these signs do you identify with? There are certainly other warning signs that precede a career transition, but those that we've mentioned generally indicate that you're up for a change. If you relate to these early-warning signs, don't wait. Do your homework now.

> *Louise Mayberry, a client of ours who had more than a few years before retirement, was facing a layoff within her organization. Louise headed the wellness program for her organization, and she realized, even before she took our "early-warning signs" quiz, that the chaos was not good for her. "Most of my colleagues were hoping to stay, so they could eventually get their retirement benefits. Not me. I went to a vice president, and made a case for putting myself on the list of those who were being asked to leave," Louise told us. "My health was at stake." She was given a very minor retirement package, set up her own business as a wellness consultant for corporations, and is much more content.*

Wanted: a gradual, no-risk career transition

If you're afraid of leaving familiar territory or taking on a challenge you don't want, we'll settle your nerves here. Our approach to career transitions is like a gentle leap to firm ground, not a haphazard jump off the nearest cliff. Granted, our approach does take some time, but it's worth the effort.

If you're in a great deal of career pain, and the warning signs are in full force, you can put all your effort into making a career transition and speed up the change. If you're just bored, a little unhappy, or a bit curious, follow the process at whatever pace is comfortable to you. Just be sure to follow it consistently. Being open to new careers or new job opportunities is a great habit to pick up.

"Better to get a stiff neck from aiming too high than a hunch back from aiming too low."
Jacques Chancel

You Might Not Get There If You Don't Know Where You Are Going

We're often asked how we motivate people to undertake a career transition which, after all, takes time and the ability to initiate and withstand change. Our answer? We don't have to motivate anybody. First of all, our clients often come to us in such career pain that they're willing to do almost anything to change careers. And second, the process we show them allows them to see where they're going. Once they have a vision of where they belong, we often have to jump out of the way. They see the end result and want to get there.

People who don't make career changes when it's clear they should, fail to make a move because they can't see where they're going. No one is willing to step off a cliff into a black abyss of uncertainty. Wouldn't you much rather have a picture of your final destination?

Understanding labor market research

We refer to the strategies you'll be choosing and the research you will be doing as labor market research. It's a whole host of techniques for getting out and researching trends in the world of work. But before you learn how to conduct labor market research, it's essential that you understand the three questions that labor market research answers. These questions are placed in a specific order for a very specific reason.

As you conduct your labor market research, you will keep uppermost in your mind the following three key questions:

1. Does this job or field interest me?
   (Do I want—or desire— to do this?)

2. What does this job or field pay?

3. What's the demand for this career field, now and in the future?

We often tell our clients to think of the questions as DPD—desire, pay, and demand. Why are they in this order? All are important, but if you can't answer yes to number one, the desire question, it doesn't matter how you answer numbers two and three. It makes no difference if the job pays $100,000 a year and will be in demand for the next fifty years. If you don't desire to do it, you won't care how much it pays or how much it's in demand. Conducting labor market research ensures that you'll find a job or career you like, one that pays well enough for you, and one that's in demand.

Labor Market Research 101

You have to first start with a grocery list of careers you're interested in and then whittle your list down to what you want and what you can get. That's the heart of labor market research. Many of our clients have certain career fields in mind that denote glamour or prestige to them, but, in reality, are nothing like what they imagine. For example, one of our clients told us, *"I've always wanted to be in public relations."* She thought it was a spectacular field to be in. But public relations isn't a *"party"* field. It actually involves writing, which isn't especially glamorous. Unless you have the ability and personality to sit down and write for hours, you don't belong in public relations.

"An objective without a plan is a dream."
Douglas McGregor

Labor market research gets you in touch with reality. It'll put your perceptions to the test. You may eliminate careers you thought were right for you and consider others you never really thought about before.

We liken the steps of labor market research to the rings of a bull's-eye. Each step gets you closer and closer to the middle—to making a career decision. The first steps are relatively easy. They provide a comfortable avenue for researching different jobs and careers. But each step requires more commitment on your part to the process, and this sometimes means leaving your comfort zone to zero in on the career or job you want. But it's the only way you'll get to your target.

"Begin difficult things while they are easy...a thousand mile journey begins with one step."
Lao Tse

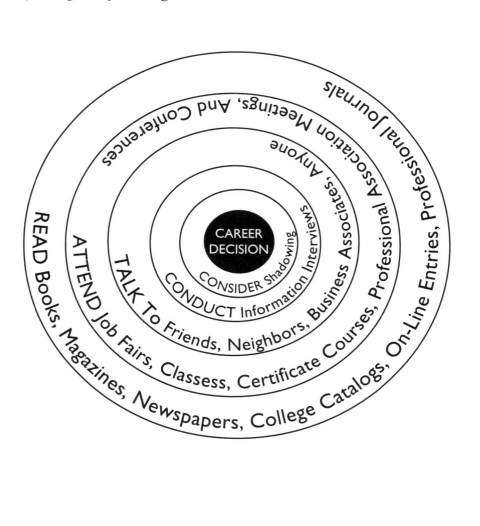

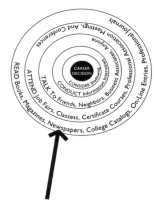

Reading is more than meets the eye

The first, easy step toward making a career decision involves research through reading. We encourage you to read books about specific careers, to explore new careers on-line, and to leaf through newspapers, magazines, college catalogs, and professional journals. It's a wonderful way to start dabbling in career information. In fact, we often advise our clients to clip *(or photocopy)* articles of interest and start files or scrapbooks of careers that appeal to them.

In this step, you're reading for interest. You're sampling careers in the broadest sense of the word. It's like checking out clothes in a magazine before you try them on and buy them; or it's comparable to reading personal ads before dating a number of people and choosing a mate. Even if you have a good idea of what you'd like to do, keep yourself open. Don't restrict yourself by narrowing down your choice to one or two job titles before you do this step.

You're reading to explore new careers, to uncover more information about one you're already thinking about, and to gather data that will allow you to make a good career decision. This data is always changing. That's why reading is on the outside of the bull's-eye. Printed material becomes dated fast. So while it's a valuable, easy way to learn about different careers, it's not the last word on the subject.

Reading about specific careers clues you in on whether or not you want to pursue those careers. It answers question number one of labor market research—Do I desire to do this? Sometimes the information given also covers pay and demand, the other two questions, but remember that your answer to question number one is of utmost importance. Read to uncover your response to that question.

All you have to do is open up a newspaper or go to the library or access journal entries on-line. Start reading what's around you. It's safe, quiet, and non threatening even to introverts. But it's not something you do only once. You must do it continually; you must constantly read and search for new information about new career fields, whether you make a transition within the next six months or the next six years.

> "Education will not simply be a prelude to a career, but a lifelong endeavor."
> Maud Barkley

Stepping Out

Careers don't quite come alive on paper. While reading is a valuable part of labor market research, this next step involves getting out of your seat and attending events that open up doors to new career opportunities. It does require more commitment on your part than reading does, but it will also get you closer to your career decision.

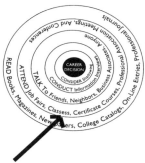

Seek out job fairs

One of the first events you may wish to attend is a job fair. We ask our clients to approach it the same way they do want ads. Job fairs rarely result in an actual job. Probably less than two percent of the people who attend a job fair get a job offer from one. So please do not go to a job fair with the expectation that you will walk out of there with a brand-new job. On the plus side, however, job fairs do offer a tremendous opportunity to do your labor market research and to practice your self-marketing skills in a safe environment.

Attend classes and certificate courses

You may also want to attend classes and certificate courses you have found in the catalogs you've been reading. The classes and certificate courses we encourage our clients to consider are typically found in the community-service catalogs or extension-course or continuing-education catalogs of colleges and universities. What you will find in these catalogs are one-day classes and certificate courses specific to certain careers. Many schools provide one-day classes in a variety of career fields.

> *A participant in one of our workshops, Ken Galbrahns, was interested in travel. Ken took a one-day course—called "Careers in Travel"—at a local college. "The course told me all the different things you could do in the travel industry, what training was needed, what money you could expect to make, and the different opportunities in the field. The instructor even helped some students write their resumes," Ken told us. "This class was worth its weight in gold. I was still interested in travel as a career, but if I hadn't been after the class, I would have only been out fifty-nine dollars, not thousands of dollars and a year or two invested in long-term training." Ken decided that the job he was interested in was that of a tour guide. "A tour guide goes on vacation with a group of twenty to twenty-five people and baby-sits them while they're on vacation. Travel is the number-one growth industry in the world, and tour guides are in great demand," Ken said. "It also pays well enough. So I answered my DPD—Desire-Pay-Demand—questions." Having taken that one-day class, Ken worked on his resume, contacted travel agencies all around the world, and got a job as a tour guide.*

Give professional associations and conferences a try

One of the quickest and easiest ways to get a picture of whether or not you'd like to be in a particular field or career is to attend a professional association meeting or conference related to that field. Most professional associations allow newcomers who aren't already a part of the field to attend meetings and conferences. However, a few elite organizations do not. For example, if you're considering becoming a doctor, you won't be welcome at an American Medical Association meeting. You have to be a doctor. Not every professional association provides easy access to career changers, but most do.

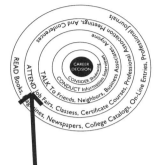

So how do you find a professional association that's connected to a career field you're interested in? Many local cities and communities have listings in the business section of their major newspapers of where the professional associations are meeting. Typically these are listed on Mondays. Also, in some communities, individuals have compiled a directory of professional associations. Check and see if one is available at your local library.

Is discovering the career for you as simple as attending meetings? Yes, it can be that easy. Many of our clients either chose careers or eliminated career choices that weren't right for them by attending professional association meetings. At an association meeting, you'll find fifty or sixty people who represent that career field. They have a collective personality. If you've ever gone to a professional association meeting, you'll know what we're talking about.

"Walk into a professional association meeting and you'll know immediately whether or not you fit in. If nobody looks or acts like you, consider it a mismatch."
Anonymous

One of our clients, Martin Ludlowe, was a high school teacher interested in finding a new career. Martin had both good teaching and program-development skills. "I was torn between training and designing training programs," he told us. Martin attended two professional association meetings. One was ASTD, the American Society for Training and Development, where people in the training field gather. The other was STC, the Society for Technical Communicators, an association for technical writers. "Visiting these two association meetings gave me a good snapshot of the two different fields," Martin said, "and helped me make a decision fairly quickly. As a more introverted person, I felt that I fit better with the members of STC. They were quieter, more analytical, and interested in technical subjects. I found my home at STC." Attending these association meetings helped Martin uncover his true career interest.

"Don't ever go into a new career with your eyes shut, because as soon as you open them, you'll be in for a big surprise. And there's no guarantee the surprise will be pleasant."
Carolyn Slater

Professional associations also host local, regional, and national conferences. As you start to get involved in a group, you'll learn about these conferences. They also are of tremendous benefit, because they provide yet another view of the career field.

Labor market research comes to life when you step out and attend job fairs, classes, and professional association meetings. You get a taste of what different career fields are like, and you can either add them to or strike them off your list of potential careers. Whatever your decision, you're learning more about what you like and don't like in a career. As we tell our clients, you have to muddle through a lot of information before you can make a clear career decision. But it's the only way to ensure the right choice.

Talking Your Way to a Good Career Decision

Yes, we're going to nudge you out of your comfort zone in this step of labor market research. Unless, that is, you love to talk to people. If you do, you'll find it easy and enjoyable. If you don't, we hope to show you the immense benefits that can result from talking to anyone and everyone about potential career fields.

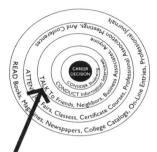

If you are interested in making a career change, you can't know too many people. Not only do you need to start talking to the people you know, but you also have to start thinking about making new friends and contacts. One of the things that got many of our clients in trouble when they needed to make a sudden change (*e.g., when they were hit with a layoff*) was that they didn't have nearly enough contacts. Or they hadn't kept up with the contacts they made.

Talking your way to a good career decision means you must be open to talking to everybody. In this step, you will certainly run into a lot of careers that you don't want to do. But that's part of the process. You just need to ask, listen, and then later determine whether or not you'd pursue that particular career choice. If you wouldn't do it even if it paid a million dollars, you'll be able to eliminate it from your list of potential careers. You will always learn something by listening to people talk about their career fields.

Where, when, and how do you start talking?

To start you thinking about where you could possibly talk about careers, consider anywhere and everywhere you go. We tell our clients to broach the career subject in grocery store lines, in your doctor's waiting room, at your kids' sporting events, on a plane, at a company softball game, at a wedding, or at a retirement dinner. You get the idea.

"Men who try to do something and fail are infinitely better off than those who try to do nothing and succeed."
Lloyd James

A client of ours, Renee Beckett, attended a golf tournament in Palm Desert and conversed with a lady behind her in the bathroom line. *"I started by talking about the weather,"* Renee said, *"and then I noticed she had a beeper on and a phone in her hand. So I said, 'You must be at work.' She was."* In fact, Renee discovered that this lady was the head of the golf tournament. She was totally in charge of the golf tournament, and she spearheaded three every year—one in Palm Desert, one in Scotland, and one in Florida. *"She makes about $75,000 a year,"* Renee told us. Such a job would never be advertised and probably never written about it. Renee got her card, and asked her permission to follow up later.

Everywhere you go, you will have mini career conversations with the people you come in contact with. After an ice breaker, you can say, *"So, what do you do?"* As your contact describes his or her job or career, you prime the pump with statements, such as, *"Oh, really? How did you get into that?"* and *"Did you get formal training for that position?"* If you're interested, you might ask the demand question: *"Is there a demand for what you do?"* And if there's a demand, you can approach the pay question by saying something like, *"If I were to consider a career in this field, what salary range would I be looking at?"*

If you're at all interested in the career, get the business card of the person you are talking to. In case the person does not have a business card, carry yours at all times. Give one of yours; then write down the name and phone number of your contact on another one of your cards.

Start talking to people. In addition to a box of business cards, you'll get career information you couldn't have gotten any other way. Certainly, you'll talk to scores of people with jobs that you'd rather not touch. But you'll also uncover some opportunities you never knew existed. And one of those careers may end up being your future career.

A Picture's Worth a Thousand Words

All of the different techniques and strategies that we've given you so far should have helped open your eyes to the very large world of work. Undoubtedly, you've seen things you'd never want to do. And, hopefully, you've also come across careers you would enjoy. Because now it's time to follow up with some of the people you've met in professional association meetings or conferences, instructors you've had in certificate courses, or the people you've met on ski lifts, in grocery stores, or at parties—the ones whose business cards you've obtained.

To actually find out whether or not the career choices you've identified are for you, you'll have to follow this last step in the labor-market research process. You'll be conducting information interviews with the people you've met, and shadowing them while they're at work. Doing these things will bring the picture of the career or careers you're considering into sharp focus.

Getting your questions answered with information interviews

An information interview is an interview to solicit information about the career field you are seriously considering. It is not—absolutely not—a job interview. We can't stress this point enough. The purpose of the information interview is to get you as close to the career field as you can without actually taking a job in it. The other technique in this step, shadowing, is a method you can use to bring you even closer to your possible career; that's why we reserve it for last. But information interviews are not optional, and they are absolutely critical to making a successful career decision.

> "If the description of a typical day at work leaves you wishing it were atypical, you need to move on."
> Anonymous

During an interview, the question that will probably get you the most information is: *"What is one of your typical days like? Can you describe it for me?"* Let us assure you that most people will tell you that they don't have a typical day. You need to respond with, *"Of course not. Tell me about yesterday."* Having them describe a typical day tells you more about that career field than almost any other question you can ask.

> *A client of ours, Amanda Hastings, went on an information interview in human resources. Like many people, Amanda thought she wanted to be in human resources because the job would have a great deal of people contact. "Well," Amanda told us, "it does and it doesn't." She interviewed a person who was an HR generalist in a small company of about three hundred employees. This person played all the HR roles. "When my contact described her typical day," Amanda said, "I discovered that the job was over 50 percent paperwork and data. The information interview brought the career into my view. I learned what I did and did not want out of human resources." Amanda did choose human resources, but she went with a much larger company and entered the area of human resources called employee relations, where you solve employee problems. "My new job has far more to do with people than the job an HR generalist does."*

Shadowing for good measure

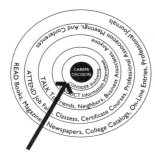

For those of you who really need to see a potential career in action, we've got one last technique. It's called shadowing. Some people never do it, and other people must do it. Shadowing is spending a minimum of two hours and a maximum of half a day with someone in a career field you think you'd like to join. In shadowing an individual, you actually watch him or her work.

Another of our clients, Marguerite Bentley, had done several information interviews in the career field of patient relations. Someone in patient relations is an ombudsman, or a troubleshooter, for the patients in a major hospital. "I really liked what I had heard in my information interviews," Marguerite told us. "I had the skills required for the job, there was a demand for it, and the pay was more than adequate. But I still thought I should watch someone in the position." So Marguerite shadowed Betty, a woman in patient relations. The first hour or so went well. "Betty first dealt with some patients who had billing problems," Marguerite explained. "Then some other patients needed help understanding what they were to do at home after they were discharged. Betty took care of them, too. But then Betty was paged and asked to come to a floor in the hospital where pandemonium reigned. Two women were having a gigantic fist fight out in the hall. Previously unknown to each other, these women were both married to a man who was dying in a nearby room. Betty had to break up the fight and arrange a visiting schedule to ensure the two families never met." Marguerite decided she didn't have the temperament to deal with such crises. However, she did eventually end up working in a hospital arranging children's programs for young inpatients. It was a much calmer career field, and it fit Marguerite's personality better.

"When you shadow people, you follow their footsteps until you know what it's like to walk in their shoes."
.Pamela Wade

We certainly realize that conducting information interviews and shadowing contacts requires effort on your part. But both provide tremendous opportunities for actually determining whether or not a career is for you. There's no better way to get a crystal-clear picture of any career.

"Procrastination is the
thief of time."
Edward Young

Pulling It All Together

Okay, we've supplied you with plenty of research ideas, techniques, and strategies. If you get good at meeting people, attending professional association meetings, and conducting information interviews, you will gather a tremendous amount of information. You'll need a way to deal with this information overload and a plan to keep you on course as you progress through each step of labor market research.

Keeping tabs on your progress

In our experience, one of the best ways to manage the mounds of information you'll be gathering is to keep a journal of your progress. At the end of every career encounter—whether it involves a stranger you met on an airplane, a professional meeting you attended, a class you took, a magazine article you read, or an information interview you conducted—as soon as you are able, you should immediately write what you liked and didn't like about what you heard, read, and/or learned. Writing down your reaction to the careers you learn about will enable you to sift through the information you receive and pull out what's important.

It may seem like extra work, but it's necessary work you do now to save time down the line. Think about it. If you happen to talk to five individuals about their careers in the course of a week, how do you expect to remember all of the details and your initial reaction to each of the careers? And what happens when, ten weeks and fifty career conversations later, you're having a hard time recalling who said what, when?

Choosing a career confidant

Another method for sorting information that we suggest to our clients is to choose a career confidant, a person with whom you can share your career reactions and impressions. Your career confidant should listen carefully and give you feedback that allows you to come to some sort of conclusion about what you're doing. However, we offer a word of advice: choose your career confidant carefully. It is best, of course, that your confidant knows you. A career confidant can't be a stranger. However, he or she also can't be somebody very close to you.

If you choose a spouse or even a co-worker, please understand that these people may have an agenda for you. By that we mean that they may or may not be thrilled about you leaving your present job and/or changing careers. Find a friend or co-worker who is enthusiastic about your change and who has no agenda for keeping you where you are.

Two of our clients, Denise Maldon and Carrie Fairfax, met at a professional association meeting—Women In Sales. "Both of us knew we were there to gather information and do labor market research," Denise said, "so we decided to form a career-change club of our own, with just the two of us as members." Together, the two decided that sales was the career field for them, and both chose to join Women In Sales. "We attended the meetings together," Carrie said, "we talked about the people we met, and we shared the names of our contacts for information interviewing and shadowing. Through the support we received from each other, we made the transition into sales." Carrie and Denise found sales jobs in different companies. "But the process for both of us was much easier because we had each other," Denise shared. "A career confidant is a tremendous boost."

A word to the wise: things do become muddier before they get clearer. As you start your labor market research, you're going to collect a bunch of data. It may take you a while to see through it all, to zero in on what you want. But we have seen, with all the thousands of clients we've worked with, that if they got out there, did their labor market research, and bounced it off their confidants and their previous assessments, they eventually discovered what it was they wanted to do. They had to sort through piles of information, but they finally settled on their vision. Perseverance was the key for them, and it will be for you also.

Coming up with a plan of action

The career-transition process works better if you set goals for yourself. Yes, we know that you may be doing your labor market research while you are currently working. But we suggest that you do something for your new career weekly—attend a meeting, take a class, or have one information interview. Get out and work on your future at least once a week. If you aren't currently working, you should be doing something every single day.

A client of ours, Myra Beaton, worked as an engineer at a major computer company. She wasn't sure whether or not she wanted to leave the company, but she was getting a little bored with the projects she was handed. "I took your advice and began doing something once a week. I first did some reading. Then I decided to broaden my horizons by attending a professional engineering association," Myra told us. "I even got very involved and joined a committee. On that committee, I met a man who was working on one of the most exciting projects I had ever heard of." Myra started to talk to the man about the details of the project, and discovered that he worked for the same company she did. "Through my contact with him," Myra said, "I made a change within my company and am very happy." She didn't know where her efforts were going to lead her, but she initiated a change, worked on it consistently, and her efforts led her right down the hall.

Managing your career in a changing workplace takes time, effort, and commitment on your part. But it's very doable, even exciting, if you know how to go about it. Our clients tell us time and again that knowing what to do makes all the difference. Learn to know yourself; market yourself; and, if a career move is in your future, follow the steps of labor market research. We wish you the best in all your career endeavors.

Summary

If you're at all interested in some sort of career change, sitting at home thinking about it won't do you any good. You have to get involved with labor market research. Read articles and journals, attend meetings and conferences, talk to everyone you can, conduct information interviews, and seriously consider shadowing. In addition, find some way to sort the information and relate it to your needs, abilities, and desires.

Since commitment to the career-transition process is vital, we also advise you to complete one activity every week, more often if you're currently out of work. And when you do change careers, keep your options open. Don't regard labor market research as a past activity. Continue reading, making contacts, attending meetings, and talking to individuals. And, if you're interested in learning more about career moves, we've included additional tips and stories in our book, *Making Career Transitions*. Check it out. Then, whenever you're ready to make another move, it'll be painless.

TITLES CURRENTLY AVAILABLE

IN THE

PERSONAL GROWTH AND DEVELOPMENT COLLECTION

Managing Your Career in a Changing Workplace

Unlocking Your Career Potential

Marketing Yourself and Your Career

Making Career Transitions

WORKSHOPS

Dynamic and interactive in-house and
public workshops are available from
Richard Chang Associates, Inc. on a
variety of personal, professional, and
organizational development topics.

ADDITIONAL RESOURCES
FROM RICHARD CHANG ASSOCIATES, INC.
PUBLICATIONS DIVISION

PRACTICAL GUIDEBOOK COLLECTION

Available through Richard Chang Associates, Inc., fine bookstores, and training and organizational development resource catalogs worldwide.

QUALITY IMPROVEMENT SERIES

Continuous Process Improvement

Continuous Improvement Tools Volume 1

Continuous Improvement Tools Volume 2

Step-By-Step Problem Solving

Meetings That Work!

Improving Through Benchmarking

Succeeding As A Self-Managed Team

Satisfying Internal Customers First!

Process Reengineering In Action

Measuring Organizational Improvement Impact

MANAGEMENT SKILLS SERIES

Coaching Through Effective Feedback

Expanding Leadership Impact

Mastering Change Management

On-The-Job Orientation And Training

Re-Creating Teams During Transitions

HIGH PERFORMANCE TEAM SERIES

Success Through Teamwork

Building A Dynamic Team

Measuring Team Performance

Team Decision-Making Techniques

HIGH-IMPACT TRAINING SERIES

Creating High-Impact Training

Identifying Targeted Training Needs

Mapping A Winning Training Approach

Producing High-Impact Learning Tools

Applying Successful Training Techniques

Measuring The Impact Of Training

Make Your Training Results Last

WORKPLACE DIVERSITY SERIES

Capitalizing On Workplace Diversity

Successful Staffing In A Diverse Workplace

Team-Building For Diverse Work Groups

Communicating In A Diverse Workplace

Tools For Valuing Diversity

TRAINING PRODUCTS

Step-By-Step Problem Solving Tool Kit

Meetings That Work! Trainer's Kit

Continuous Improvement Tools Volume 1 Trainer's Kit

101 Stupid Things Trainers Do To Sabotage Success

VIDEOTAPES

Mastering Change Management**

Quality: You Don't Have To Be Sick To Get Better*

Achieving Results Through Quality Improvement*

Total Quality: Myths, Methods, Or Miracles**
  Featuring Drs. Ken Blanchard and Richard Chang

Empowering The Quality Effort**
  Featuring Drs. Ken Blanchard and Richard Chang

* Produced by American Media Inc.

TOTAL QUALITY VIDEO SERIES AND WORKBOOKS

Building Commitment**

Teaming Up**

Applied Problem Solving**

Self-Directed Evaluation**

** Produced by Double Vision Studios

EVALUATION AND FEEDBACK FORM

We need your help to continuously improve the quality of the resources provided through the Richard Chang Associates, Inc., Publications Division. We would greatly appreciate your input and suggestions regarding this particular book, as well as future book interests.

Thank you in advance for your feedback.

Title: _____

1. Overall, how would you rate your *level of satisfaction* with this book? Please circle your response.

   Extremely Dissatisfied   Satisfied   Extremely Satisfied

         1   2   3   4   5

2. What did you find *most* helpful?

   _____

   _____

3. What did you find *least* helpful?

   _____

   _____

4. What *characteristics/features/benefits* are most important to you in making a decision to purchase a book?

   _____

   _____

5. What additional *subject matter/topic areas* would you like to see addressed in future books from Richard Chang Associates, Inc.?

   _____

   _____

Name *(optional)*:_____

Address: _____

C/S/Z: _____   **Phone:** ( ) _____

PLEASE FAX YOUR RESPONSES TO: (714) 727-7007
OR MAIL YOUR RESPONSE TO: RICHARD CHANG ASSOCIATES, INC.
15265 ALTON PARKWAY, SUITE 300, IRVINE, CA 92618
OR CALL US AT: (800) 756-8096

RAP

GAYLORD F